Trump's Insurrection of the US Capitol

Adrian Rocquecliffe

Published by Writers Sidekick Publishing, 2024.

While every precaution has been taken in the preparation of this book, the publisher assumes no responsibility for errors or omissions, or for damages resulting from the use of the information contained herein.

TRUMP'S INSURRECTION OF THE US CAPITOL

First edition. July 16, 2024.

ISBN: 979-8227431523

Written by Adrian Rocquecliffe.

INSURRECTION AT THE U.S. CAPITOL

January 6, 2021, Insurrection At The U.S. Capitol

January 6, 2021, will be remembered as a dark and unprecedented chapter in American history. On that day, as Congress convened to certify the results of the 2020 presidential election, a violent insurrection unfolded at the U.S. Capitol, leaving a lasting scar on the nation's democratic institutions.

The insurrection began as a rally organized by supporters of then-President Donald Trump, who had refused to concede defeat in the election and had spent weeks spreading baseless claims of voter fraud. As Trump addressed his followers, he repeated his false assertions about the election being stolen. He urged his supporters to "fight like hell" to overturn the results.

Following Trump's speech, thousands of his supporters marched to the Capitol, where lawmakers were certifying the Electoral College vote. What began as a protest quickly escalated into chaos and violence as the mob breached security barriers and stormed the Capitol building, breaking windows, vandalizing offices, and clashing with law enforcement officers.

Inside the Capitol, lawmakers and staff were forced to evacuate or shelter in place as the mob roamed the halls, chanting slogans and brandishing weapons. The scenes of chaos and destruction broadcast live on television shocked the nation and drew condemnation from leaders worldwide.

The insurrection resulted in multiple deaths, including Capitol Police Officer Brian Sicknick, who was fatally injured while defending the building, and four others who died as a result of the violence. Dozens of law enforcement officers were also injured in the melee.

The attempted coup ultimately failed to overturn the election results, as Congress reconvened later that evening to complete the certification process. However, the insurrection laid bare the deep divisions and political polarization that have plagued American society in recent years and the dangers posed by the spread of disinformation and conspiracy theories.

In the aftermath of the insurrection, Trump was impeached by the House of Representatives for incitement of insurrection, making him the first president in U.S. history to be impeached twice. The Senate later acquitted him, but the events of January 6 cast a long shadow over his presidency and further tarnished his legacy.

The January 6 insurrection serves as a stark reminder of the fragility of democracy and the importance of upholding democratic norms and institutions. It was a day that will be remembered as a dark chapter in American history, a moment when the peaceful transfer of power was threatened by violence and lawlessness.

Context

In the weeks leading up to January 6, 2021, tensions in the United States reached a boiling point following the contentious presidential election. Despite widespread acknowledgment of Joe Biden's victory, then-President Donald Trump refused to accept the outcome, claiming without evidence that the election had been marred by widespread fraud and irregularities.

Trump and his allies relentlessly promoted baseless conspiracy theories, alleging that the election had been "stolen" from him through fraudulent means. These claims were repeatedly debunked by election officials, courts, and independent observers, who found no evidence of widespread voter fraud or irregularities that would have affected the election outcome.

Despite these debunkings, Trump continued to spread misinformation and sow doubt about the integrity of the electoral process, further polarizing the country and deepening divisions among Americans. His refusal to concede defeat and his efforts to overturn the election results fueled anger and resentment among his supporters, many of whom felt disenfranchised and betrayed by the outcome of the election.

On January 6, Trump escalated his campaign to overturn the election results by calling his supporters to come to Washington, D.C., for a rally near the White House. In the days leading up to the event, he used his social media platforms to promote the rally and encourage his followers to attend, promising it would be a historic event.

At the rally on January 6, Trump delivered a fiery speech in which he reiterated his false claims of voter fraud and insisted that the election had been "stolen" from him. He urged his supporters to "fight like hell" to overturn the results and vowed never to concede defeat.

Trump's rhetoric at the rally was combative and provocative, as he encouraged his supporters to march to the Capitol and show strength in protesting the certification of the Electoral College vote. He told them that if they didn't "fight like hell," they wouldn't have a country anymore.

Following Trump's speech, thousands of his supporters marched to the Capitol, where Congress was certifying the Electoral College vote. What began as a protest quickly descended into chaos and violence as the mob breached security barriers and stormed the Capitol building, disrupting the certification process and forcing lawmakers to evacuate.

The events of January 6 shocked the nation. They reverberated around the world, exposing the fragility of American democracy and the dangers of political polarization and misinformation. The insurrection at the Capitol was a dark and unprecedented chapter in American history, one that underscored the urgent need to confront the forces of extremism and division that threaten the foundations of democracy.

Rally Speech

During the rally preceding the January 6 insurrection, then-President Donald Trump delivered a speech that further inflamed the already charged atmosphere among his supporters. In his address, Trump reiterated his baseless claims of election fraud and insisted that the 2020 presidential election had been "stolen" from him. Despite lacking any evidence to support his allegations, he continued to propagate falsehoods about the integrity of the electoral process.

Trump's rhetoric at the rally was characterized by its inflammatory nature, as he urged his supporters to take action to overturn the election results. He used language that could be interpreted as incitement, telling the crowd to "fight like hell" and suggesting that their actions would determine the fate of the nation. This language was interpreted by many as a call to engage in aggressive and potentially violent behavior.

Moreover, Trump specifically directed his supporters to march to the Capitol and "take back our country." This directive was particularly concerning given the context of the rally, where thousands of his supporters had gathered in Washington, D.C., and tensions were running high.

By encouraging his supporters to march on the Capitol and suggesting that their actions could change the outcome of the election, Trump effectively escalated the situation and contributed to the atmosphere of unrest and chaos that ultimately led to the violent insurrection at the Capitol later that day.

Critics argued that Trump's rally speech was reckless and irresponsible, as it fueled the anger and resentment of his supporters and helped incite the violent attack on the Capitol. His words were seen as a clear example of his willingness to prioritize his political interests over the safety and stability of the nation, further eroding public trust in the democratic process.

Storming of the Capitol

After Donald Trump's fiery rally speech on January 6, 2021, thousands of his supporters marched from the rally site to the U.S. Capitol, where a joint session of Congress was convened to certify the Electoral College results affirming Joe Biden's victory in the 2020 presidential election. What began as a protest quickly devolved into chaos and violence as the mob breached security barriers and overwhelmed law enforcement officers stationed outside the Capitol building.

Despite the presence of Capitol Police and other law enforcement agencies, the mob managed to forcibly enter the Capitol complex, breaking windows, vandalizing property, and engaging in confrontations with law enforcement personnel. The scenes of rioters storming the Capitol, some armed with weapons and others carrying Confederate flags or wearing clothing with white supremacist symbols, shocked the nation and drew condemnation from leaders across the political spectrum.

Inside the Capitol, lawmakers and staff were evacuated to secure locations as the rioters roamed the halls, chanting slogans and ransacking offices. The violence resulted in multiple deaths and injuries, including the fatal shooting of a protester by law enforcement and the deaths of several others due to medical emergencies.

The storming of the Capitol was a bold and unprecedented attack on American democracy, as rioters sought to disrupt the constitutional process of certifying the Electoral College results and overturn the outcome of a free and fair election. The images of the chaos and destruction broadcast around the world underscored the fragility of democratic institutions and the dangers of political extremism.

The January 6, 2021, events will be remembered as a dark chapter in American history, a stark reminder of the consequences of political polarization, disinformation, and the erosion of democratic norms. The insurrection at the Capitol laid bare the deep divisions within American society and the urgent need to address the underlying factors that contributed to the violence and unrest.

Violent Confrontations

The events of January 6, 2021, at the United States Capitol unfolded into a scene of unprecedented chaos and violence. As supporters of then-President Donald Trump breached the Capitol building, they engaged in confrontations with law enforcement officers and congressional staff. Rioters, fueled by anger and misinformation about the outcome of the 2020 presidential election, pushed through barricades and overwhelmed security forces, allowing them to enter the Capitol complex.

Once inside, the rioters unleashed a wave of violence and destruction. They roamed the halls of the Capitol, shouting slogans, waving flags, and brandishing weapons. The scene was chaotic and surreal as rioters occupied congressional offices, vandalized property, and clashed with law enforcement personnel. The Capitol was placed on lockdown, and the proceedings of the electoral vote certification were abruptly halted as members of Congress were evacuated or sheltered in place to ensure their safety.

The violent confrontations between the rioters and law enforcement officers resulted in injuries and casualties. Both Capitol Police officers and rioters sustained injuries during the clashes, and tragically, several lives were lost as a result of the violence. The events of January 6 shocked the nation and reverberated worldwide, prompting widespread condemnation and calls for accountability.

The breach of the Capitol, a symbol of American democracy, was an unprecedented assault on the foundations of the nation's political system. The violent insurrection aimed to disrupt the peaceful transfer of power and overturn the results of a free and fair election. The scenes of chaos and destruction underscored the fragility of democratic institutions and the dangers of political extremism.

In the aftermath of the Capitol attack, law enforcement agencies launched extensive investigations to identify and prosecute those responsible for inciting and participating in the violence. The events of January 6 served as a stark reminder of the importance of upholding the rule of law, defending democratic principles, and safeguarding the integrity of the electoral process.

Desecration of Symbols of Democracy

The desecration of symbols of democracy during the events of January 6, 2021, at the United States Capitol was a shocking display of lawlessness and contempt for the principles of American governance. Rioters, incited by false claims of election fraud and goaded by then-President Donald Trump, engaged in acts of vandalism and destruction as they stormed the Capitol building.

Inside the Capitol, rioters targeted critical symbols of American democracy with daring acts of disrespect and aggression. The mob breached the Senate chamber, where the nation's lawmakers convene to debate and legislate. Rioters roamed freely through the hallowed halls, defacing property and looting offices. Speaker Nancy Pelosi's office, a symbol of congressional leadership, was among the spaces vandalized by the insurrectionists. Furniture was overturned, documents were scattered, and personal belongings were ransacked in a display of lawlessness and chaos.

Outside the Capitol, the scene was equally disturbing. Rioters erected gallows on the Capitol grounds, evoking images of lynching and violence. Confederate flags, a symbol of racism and oppression, were proudly displayed alongside other emblems of white supremacy. The presence of such symbols sent a chilling message and underscored the deeply troubling motivations behind the insurrection.

In addition to physical destruction, the rioters engaged in vile and despicable behavior, including smearing feces on the walls of the Capitol and leaving threatening messages for lawmakers. These grotesque acts of vandalism were intended to instill fear and intimidation among elected officials. They underscored the violent and extremist nature of the insurrection.

The desecration of symbols of democracy during the Capitol attack was a direct assault on the foundations of American governance. It represented an affront to the principles of freedom, equality, and justice upon which the nation was founded. The scenes of destruction and disrespect shocked the nation and drew condemnation from leaders across the political spectrum.

In the aftermath of the insurrection, efforts were made to restore and repair the damage inflicted on the Capitol building. However, the scars left by the events of January 6 serve as a sobering reminder of the fragility of democracy and the ongoing struggle to uphold its principles in the face of extremism and violence.

Loss of Life and Injuries

The insurrection at the United States Capitol on January 6, 2021, resulted in a tragic loss of life and numerous injuries, marking one of the darkest days in American history. As rioters stormed the Capitol building in a violent attempt to overturn the results of the 2020 presidential election, the chaos and lawlessness led to devastating consequences.

Among the casualties was a Capitol Police officer, Brian Sicknick, who tragically lost his life in the line of duty. Officer Sicknick was fatally injured while engaging with the mob, reportedly suffering from injuries sustained during physical altercations with rioters. His death sent shockwaves through the nation and underscored the extreme dangers faced by law enforcement officers tasked with protecting the Capitol and those inside.

In addition to Officer Sicknick, four others lost their lives during the insurrection, including a woman who was shot by law enforcement as she attempted to breach a barricaded area within the Capitol building. The loss of life was a sobering reminder of the deadly consequences of political violence and extremism.

Beyond the fatalities, the insurrection resulted in numerous injuries to both law enforcement officers and protesters. Dozens of Capitol Police officers were injured during the violent clashes, suffering from injuries ranging from concussions to broken bones as they attempted to repel the mob and defend the Capitol complex. Rioters also sustained injuries during the chaotic melee, with reports of individuals being trampled, struck by projectiles, or injured in altercations with law enforcement.

The loss of life and injuries sustained during the insurrection served as a stark reminder of the real-world consequences of political violence and the urgent need to address the underlying factors fueling extremism and polarization in American society. The tragic events of January 6 left a scar on the nation's conscience. They underscored the importance of defending democratic principles and institutions against those who seek to undermine them through violence and insurrection.

Delayed Certification Process

The attack on the United States Capitol on January 6, 2021, had profound implications for the certification process of the Electoral College results, which was underway at the time of the insurrection. As the violent mob breached the Capitol building, lawmakers were forced to evacuate and seek shelter to ensure their safety, bringing the proceedings to a grinding halt.

The certification process, a routine and constitutionally mandated procedure, was abruptly interrupted by the unprecedented chaos and violence unfolding within the Capitol complex. The joint session of Congress convened to count and certify the Electoral College votes was suspended as rioters clashed with law enforcement officers and roamed the halls of the Capitol.

The certification process remained in limbo for several hours as law enforcement authorities worked to secure the Capitol and restore order. Meanwhile, lawmakers, staff, and other individuals inside the Capitol were evacuated to safety, sheltering in undisclosed locations to avoid the violent mob.

Despite the disruption and chaos, the resilience of American democracy prevailed. Order was eventually restored, and Congress reconvened to fulfill its constitutional duty to certify the Electoral College results. In a defiant display of unity and resolve, lawmakers returned to the Capitol to complete the certification process, reaffirming the outcome of the 2020 presidential election.

After a brief debate and deliberation, Congress formally certified Joe Biden's victory as the next President of the United States, affirming his electoral win over then-President Donald Trump. The certification of the Electoral

College results marked a crucial moment in the peaceful transition of power, underscoring the strength of American democracy and its ability to withstand even the most severe challenges.

The delayed certification process served as a stark reminder of the fragility of democratic institutions and the importance of upholding the rule of law in the face of political violence and extremism. Despite the unprecedented disruption caused by the insurrection, the certification of Joe Biden's victory signaled a reaffirmation of democratic norms and a commitment to the peaceful transfer of power, ultimately ensuring the continuity of American governance.

Impeachment and Consequences

In the aftermath of the violent insurrection at the United States Capitol on January 6, 2021, then-President Donald Trump faced swift and widespread condemnation from across the political spectrum. Lawmakers, both Democrats and Republicans, held Trump accountable for his role in inciting the violence that led to the breach of the Capitol building. Trump's actions including his repeated false claims of election fraud and his fiery rhetoric urging supporters to "fight like hell" to overturn the election results - were seen as contributing to the atmosphere of anger and unrest that culminated in the attack on the Capitol.

In response to Trump's perceived blame for the insurrection, the House of Representatives moved quickly to impeach him for "incitement of insurrection." This historic second impeachment made Trump the first president in U.S. history to be impeached twice. The impeachment proceedings were characterized by impassioned debates and stark divisions along party lines, reflecting the deep-seated political polarization gripping the nation.

Despite the House's decision to impeach Trump, the subsequent Senate trial ended in an acquittal and set free. While a bipartisan group of senators voted to convict Trump, the majority fell short of the two-thirds threshold required for conviction. The acquittal disappointed many who believed that Trump should be held accountable for his actions. However, it also underscored the challenges of achieving consensus in a deeply divided political environment.

Although Trump was acquitted in the Senate trial, the events of January 6 had lasting consequences for his political legacy and the country's democratic institutions. The insurrection laid bare the dangers of political extremism and the potential for violence when leaders peddle false narratives and sow division for personal gain. The attack on the Capitol shocked the nation. It prompted soul-searching about the state of American democracy, leading to calls for accountability and reform.

In the months following the insurrection, Trump's influence within the Republican Party remained strong. However, fractures emerged as some GOP lawmakers distanced themselves from his rhetoric and actions. The events of January 6 prompted a reckoning within the party about its direction and values as Republicans grappled with how to move forward in the post-Trump era.

While Trump may have avoided immediate consequences through the Senate's acquittal, the insurrection and its aftermath left an indelible mark on American politics. The events of January 6 served as a stark reminder of the fragility of democracy and the imperative of upholding democratic norms and institutions in the face of threats from within and without.

Law Enforcement Response

The law enforcement response to the breach of the U.S. Capitol on January 6, 2021, was met with widespread criticism for its perceived inadequacy and lack of preparedness. Despite warnings of potential violence and the presence of a large, agitated crowd gathered near the Capitol complex, Capitol Police appeared ill-equipped. They were overwhelmed by the scale of the insurrection that unfolded.

In the days leading up to January 6, there were numerous indications that extremist groups and supporters of then-President Donald Trump were planning to converge on Washington, D.C., to protest the certification of the Electoral College results. Social media platforms were rife with threats of violence and calls for action, prompting concerns among law enforcement agencies and government officials about the potential for unrest.

Despite these warnings, the response from law enforcement on the day of the insurrection appeared disjointed and uncoordinated. As rioters breached barricades and stormed the Capitol building, Capitol Police officers initially struggled to contain the mob and protect the perimeter of the complex. Videos and eyewitness accounts from the scene depicted chaotic scenes of officers being overrun by the crowd, leading to scenes of violence and destruction.

The apparent lack of preparation and coordination between law enforcement agencies also came under scrutiny in the aftermath of the insurrection. Despite the clear and present threat posed by the gathering crowd, there were delays in deploying additional resources and reinforcements to secure the Capitol and restore order. Questions were raised about the chain of command, communication protocols, and decision-making processes within law enforcement agencies tasked with protecting the Capitol and those inside.

In the wake of the insurrection, there were calls for a thorough investigation into the law enforcement response and accountability for any failures or lapses that contributed to the breach of the Capitol. Congressional hearings and inquiries sought to uncover the factors that led to the breakdown in security and identify steps to prevent similar incidents.

The law enforcement response to the January 6 insurrection was criticized for its shortcomings and failures. The breach of the Capitol exposed vulnerabilities in the security infrastructure. It raised serious questions about the ability of law enforcement agencies to handle threats to the democratic process. As the nation grappled with the aftermath of the attack, there was a renewed focus on the need for reform and improvements to ensure the safety and security of government institutions and those who serve within them.

Political Fallout

The events of January 6, 2021, reverberated throughout the political landscape of the United States, exacerbating already deep-seated divisions and sparking widespread condemnation from lawmakers on both sides of the aisle. The brazen attack on the U.S. Capitol, the seat of American democracy, sent shockwaves across the nation and prompted a swift and unequivocal response from political leaders at all levels of government.

In the immediate aftermath of the insurrection, lawmakers from both parties condemned the violence in no uncertain terms, expressing alarm and outrage at the attack on the heart of American democracy. Democrats and Republicans alike spoke out against the assault on the Capitol, with many describing it as an assault on the very foundations of democracy and an affront to the rule of law.

The insurrection also prompted calls for accountability and investigations into the security failures that allowed it to occur, as well as the role of political leaders in inciting the violence. Lawmakers vowed to conduct thorough inquiries to uncover the root causes of the attack and identify those responsible for orchestrating and carrying it out. Congressional hearings and investigations were launched to examine the breakdown in security at the Capitol and assess the adequacy of law enforcement response.

Additionally, there were calls for accountability for political leaders perceived to have contributed to the division and unrest that culminated in the insurrection. Many lawmakers and public officials pointed fingers at then-President Donald Trump, accusing him of inciting the violence with his inflammatory rhetoric and baseless claims of election fraud. Trump's role in stoking tensions and encouraging his supporters to "fight like hell" to overturn the election results came under intense scrutiny, leading to his second impeachment by the House of Representatives.

The political fallout from the January 6 insurrection was profound, further deepening the rifts within American society and raising questions about the future of democracy in the United States. The attack laid bare the extent of political polarization and extremism in the country, highlighting the urgent need for unity, reconciliation, and reform. As the nation grappled with the aftermath of the insurrection, political leaders faced the daunting task of restoring faith in democratic institutions and healing the wounds inflicted by one of the darkest days in American history.

Impact on Global Perception

The insurrection at the U.S. Capitol on January 6, 2021, had far-reaching implications beyond American borders, sending shockwaves throughout the international community and casting doubt on America's reputation as a bastion of democracy and stability. The scenes of chaos and violence that unfolded in the heart of the nation's capital were broadcast around the world, leaving a lasting impression and prompting widespread concern about the state of democracy in the United States.

For allies and adversaries alike, the events of January 6 were met with disbelief and condemnation. Countries that have long looked to the United States as a beacon of democracy and freedom were dismayed by the scenes of mob violence and the assault on democratic institutions. The sight of rioters breaching the Capitol and disrupting the peaceful transfer of power sent a chilling message about the fragility of democracy and the potential for political instability, even in the world's oldest democracy.

The global perception of the United States was tarnished by the insurrection, with many questioning America's commitment to democratic principles and the rule of law. The images of Confederate flags and other symbols of hate and extremism being brandished inside the Capitol fueled concerns about the rise of domestic extremism and the erosion of democratic norms in the United States.

Adversaries of the United States seized on the chaos and violence to sow doubt and undermine confidence in American democracy. Authoritarian regimes and anti-democratic forces pointed to the events of January 6 as evidence of the inherent weaknesses of democracy and the dangers of political dissent. They used the insurrection as propaganda to discredit the United States and advance their agendas on the world stage.

The impact of the insurrection on global perception was profound and enduring, with ramifications for America's standing in the world and its ability to promote democracy and human rights abroad. In the wake of the attack, there were calls for soul-searching and introspection about the state of democracy in the United States and the need to address the underlying factors contributing to the breakdown of democratic norms and institutions.

Ultimately, the insurrection at the U.S. Capitol served as a wake-up call for the international community, highlighting the importance of defending democratic values and institutions against threats from within and without. It underscored the fragility of democracy and the need for constant vigilance to safeguard the principles that lie at the heart of free and open societies worldwide.

National Guard Deployment

In response to the escalating violence and chaos unfolding at the U.S. Capitol on January 6, 2021, authorities swiftly mobilized the D.C. National Guard and other law enforcement agencies to restore order and secure the area. The deployment of the National Guard marked a significant escalation in the government's response to the insurrection and underscored the severity of the situation.

As the situation at the Capitol deteriorated and rioters breached the building, it became clear that additional reinforcements were needed to quell the violence and protect lawmakers, staff, and other individuals inside. In coordination with federal and state authorities, the D.C. National Guard was activated and deployed to the Capitol complex to bolster security and assist in the response efforts.

The deployment of the National Guard was a critical step in restoring order and ensuring the safety of those present at the Capitol. National Guard troops, equipped with riot gear and other tactical equipment, worked alongside Capitol Police and other law enforcement agencies to secure the perimeter of the Capitol, evacuate individuals from the building, and contain the violent mob.

In addition to the National Guard, additional law enforcement resources were mobilized to assist in the response efforts. Federal agencies, including the FBI, Department of Homeland Security, and Secret Service, provided support and expertise in managing the crisis and investigating the events leading up to the insurrection.

The deployment of the National Guard and other law enforcement agencies marked a decisive response to the unprecedented attack on the Capitol. It underscored the government's commitment to upholding the rule of law and defending democratic institutions. It also served as a stark reminder of the importance of maintaining readiness and preparedness to respond to threats to public safety and national security.

Overall, the deployment of the National Guard played a crucial role in restoring order and preventing further violence at the U.S. Capitol. It demonstrated the effectiveness of coordinated response efforts and the dedication of law enforcement personnel to protecting the nation's capital and safeguarding the democratic process.

Social Media's Role

The events of January 6, 2021, shed a harsh spotlight on the role of social media platforms in shaping public discourse, amplifying misinformation, and facilitating the spread of extremist ideologies. In the lead-up to the insurrection, social media played a central role in disseminating false claims of election fraud and galvanizing supporters of then-President Donald Trump to rally in Washington, D.C.

For months leading up to January 6, Trump and his allies used social media platforms such as Twitter, Facebook, and YouTube to propagate baseless allegations of widespread voter fraud in the 2020 presidential election. Despite being repeatedly debunked by election officials and courts, these claims gained traction among Trump's supporters and fueled distrust in the electoral process.

Social media platforms served as a powerful megaphone for Trump and his allies to mobilize supporters and organize the "Stop the Steal" rally in Washington, D.C., on January 6. Posts and messages promoting the rally circulated widely on platforms like Facebook, Twitter, and Parler, attracting thousands of attendees who converged on the Capitol to protest the certification of the Electoral College results.

Social media played a dual role during the insurrection, documenting the chaos unfolding in real-time and potentially exacerbating the violence. Rioters livestreamed their actions on platforms like Facebook and YouTube, providing a chilling glimpse into the mayhem inside the Capitol. At the same time, false information and conspiracy theories spread rapidly on social media, further inflaming tensions and fueling the unrest.

In the aftermath of the insurrection, social media companies faced intense scrutiny and criticism for their role in amplifying misinformation and extremism. Platforms such as Twitter, Facebook, and YouTube took swift action to remove posts and accounts linked to the violence and suspend or ban users who violated their policies against inciting violence and spreading false information.

The events of January 6 prompted calls for accountability and regulation of social media platforms to curb the spread of misinformation and extremism. Lawmakers and public officials called for reforms to address the unchecked power of tech giants and ensure greater transparency and accountability in how they moderate content and enforce their policies.

Overall, the insurrection at the U.S. Capitol highlighted the profound impact of social media on political discourse and public safety. It underscored the need for greater scrutiny and regulation of social media platforms to prevent the spread of misinformation and extremism, protect democratic institutions, and safeguard public trust in the electoral process.

Security Measures and Investigations

Following the insurrection at the U.S. Capitol on January 6, 2021, comprehensive security measures were implemented to prevent further violence and safeguard the Capitol complex. In response to the unprecedented security breach, barriers were erected, and a substantial law enforcement presence was maintained to deter potential threats and ensure the safety of lawmakers, staff, and visitors.

The heightened security measures included deploying additional law enforcement personnel, including members of the National Guard and federal agencies, to reinforce the perimeter of the Capitol and bolster security checkpoints. Physical barriers such as fencing and concrete were erected around the Capitol complex to restrict access and prevent unauthorized entry.

In addition to the visible security presence, enhanced security protocols were implemented, including increased surveillance and intelligence monitoring to detect and respond to potential threats in real time. Capitol Police and other law enforcement agencies collaborated to coordinate response efforts and maintain situational awareness of emerging threats.

Concurrently, multiple investigations were launched to identify and hold accountable those responsible for the attack on the Capitol. Federal authorities, including the FBI and Department of Justice, spearheaded efforts to identify and apprehend individuals involved in the insurrection, leveraging surveillance footage, social media posts, and tips from the public to track down suspects.

The investigations resulted in hundreds of arrests and charges against individuals implicated in the insurrection, including offenses such as trespassing, assault, vandalism, and conspiracy. Law enforcement agencies worked diligently to build cases against perpetrators and bring them to justice, demonstrating a commitment to holding accountable those who sought to undermine democracy and engage in acts of violence and insurrection.

The investigations into the January 6 insurrection remain ongoing, with authorities continuing to pursue leads and identify additional suspects involved in the attack. The prosecutions of individuals charged in connection with the insurrection serve as a critical step in upholding the rule of law and ensuring accountability for those responsible for the assault on the Capitol and the democratic process.

Overall, the security measures and investigations undertaken in the aftermath of the insurrection underscored the government's commitment to protecting democratic institutions and preserving the integrity of the Capitol. While significant challenges remain in addressing the underlying factors that led to the attack, the response to January 6 demonstrated the resilience of American democracy and the determination of law enforcement to uphold the rule of law in the face of adversity.

Reckoning with Extremism

The insurrection at the U.S. Capitol on January 6, 2021, served as a stark wake-up call to the growing threat of extremism and domestic terrorism in the United States. The brazen attack, fueled by baseless conspiracy theories and false claims of election fraud, underscored the dangers posed by right-wing extremism and violent extremist groups.

In the aftermath of the insurrection, law enforcement agencies and policymakers across the country grappled with the urgent need to confront and address the rise of extremism. The attack prompted soul-searching and reflection on the factors that contributed to the radicalization of individuals and the escalation of violence.

One of the critical challenges facing authorities was identifying and dismantling extremist networks and organizations operating within the United States. Law enforcement agencies launched investigations into extremist groups and individuals involved in the insurrection, aiming to disrupt their activities and hold them accountable for their actions.

At the same time, there was a growing recognition of the need for a holistic approach to combating extremism, one that addresses the underlying grievances and vulnerabilities that make individuals susceptible to radicalization. Efforts to address the root causes of extremism included initiatives to promote social cohesion, strengthen community resilience, and address socioeconomic inequalities that can fuel feelings of disenfranchisement and alienation.

Additionally, there were calls for greater coordination and cooperation among law enforcement agencies, government agencies, and civil society organizations to share information, resources, and best practices in countering extremism. Multidisciplinary approaches involving law enforcement, mental health professionals, educators, and community leaders were seen as essential in preventing radicalization and intervening with individuals at risk of engaging in extremist behavior.

The insurrection also prompted a broader conversation about the role of technology and social media platforms in amplifying extremist rhetoric and facilitating recruitment and radicalization. There were calls for greater accountability and regulation of online platforms to curb the spread of hate speech and disinformation and prevent extremists from using these platforms to organize and incite violence.

Overall, the insurrection at the U.S. Capitol catalyzed a renewed focus on combating extremism and domestic terrorism in the United States. While significant challenges remain in addressing the complex and multifaceted nature of the threat, the events of January 6 underscored the need for sustained and concerted efforts to strengthen resilience against radicalization and violence and uphold the values of democracy, tolerance, and pluralism.

Symbolism and Significance

The attack on the U.S. Capitol on January 6, 2021, reverberated far beyond the halls of Congress, sending shockwaves through the country and the world. The breach of the Capitol, a revered symbol of American democracy and governance, struck the heart of the nation's democratic institutions and values, shaking the foundation of trust in the peaceful transfer of power and the rule of law.

The symbolism of the Capitol, with its iconic dome and grand architecture, holds deep historical significance as a beacon of democracy and freedom, representing the ideals upon which the United States was founded. The sight of rioters breaching the Capitol and disrupting the proceedings to certify the Electoral College results was a profound and chilling moment, evoking images of political upheaval and instability more commonly associated with authoritarian regimes.

The attack on the Capitol represented a direct assault on the institutions and principles that underpin American democracy. By storming the Capitol and seeking to disrupt the certification of the election results, the insurrectionists sought to undermine the legitimacy of the electoral process and overturn the will of the voters, striking at the core of democratic governance.

Moreover, the breach of the Capitol served as a stark reminder of the fragility of democracy and the need for constant vigilance in defending it against foreign and domestic threats. The events of January 6 exposed vulnerabilities in the security of the Capitol and raised questions about the resilience of democratic institutions in the face of concerted efforts to undermine them.

The symbolism of the Capitol attack reverberated around the world, eliciting shock and condemnation from allies and adversaries alike. The sight of the seat of American democracy under siege sent a sobering message about the challenges facing democracies in an era of rising authoritarianism and political polarization.

In the aftermath of the insurrection, there was a renewed sense of urgency and determination to defend democratic values and institutions against threats posed by extremism, disinformation, and political violence. The attack on the Capitol served as a rallying cry for unity and resilience in the face of adversity, reaffirming the enduring strength of American democracy and the commitment of its people to uphold the principles of freedom, justice, and equality for all.

Impeachment Proceedings

The impeachment proceedings that unfolded in the wake of the January 6 insurrection at the U.S. Capitol marked a historic moment in American politics, underscoring the gravity of the attack and the accountability of political leaders for their actions. The House of Representatives wasted no time in taking action, swiftly impeaching then-President Donald Trump for a second time on the charge of "incitement of insurrection."

The decision to impeach Trump reflected the severity of the events that transpired on January 6 and the consensus among lawmakers that Trump bore responsibility for inciting the violence that erupted at the Capitol. The articles of impeachment accused Trump of encouraging his supporters to storm the Capitol to overturn the results of the 2020 presidential election, which he had repeatedly falsely claimed was stolen from him.

The impeachment proceedings unfolded against the backdrop of heightened tensions and political divisions, with Democrats and some Republicans calling for accountability and consequences for Trump's role in fomenting unrest. The House vote to impeach Trump, which garnered bipartisan support, sent a powerful message about the importance of holding elected officials accountable for their actions, even in the waning days of a presidency.

However, the Senate trial presented a more challenging path to conviction, as it occurred after Trump had left office and was no longer serving as president. Despite compelling evidence presented by House impeachment managers and emotional testimony from witnesses, the Senate ultimately acquitted Trump of the charges against him, falling short of the two-thirds majority needed for conviction.

The outcome of the impeachment trial was met with disappointment and frustration by many who had hoped to see Trump held accountable for his role in inciting the insurrection. Critics argued that the acquittal sent the wrong message about the consequences of political violence and failed to address the underlying issues of extremism and polarization that contributed to the attack on the Capitol.

Nevertheless, the impeachment proceedings reckoned with the events of January 6 and the broader implications for American democracy. They underscored the importance of upholding the rule of law and the integrity of the electoral process while raising questions about the limits of presidential power and the responsibilities of political leaders in promoting unity and stability. Despite Trump's acquittal, the impeachment proceedings left an indelible mark on his presidency and the legacy of the January 6 insurrection, shaping public perception and the trajectory of American politics for years to come.

Historical Parallels

The insurrection at the U.S. Capitol on January 6, 2021, sparked comparisons to pivotal political violence and upheaval in American history, drawing parallels to events such as the Civil War and the War of 1812. While the breach of the Capitol was unprecedented in modern times, it evoked themes of sedition, rebellion, and domestic terrorism that have surfaced at critical junctures in the nation's past.

The insurrection at the Capitol brought to mind the tumultuous period leading up to the Civil War when the nation was sharply divided over issues of slavery, states' rights, and the future of the Union. The attack on the Capitol, fueled by grievances and misinformation, echoed the secessionist sentiments and acts of violence that ultimately led to the deadliest conflict in American history. The imagery of Confederate flags and symbols of white supremacy among the insurrectionists further underscored the echoes of the Civil War era and the enduring legacy of racial divisions in American society.

Similarly, the events of January 6 evoked memories of the War of 1812, when British forces invaded Washington, D.C., and set fire to the Capitol and other government buildings. The attack on the Capitol by a hostile foreign power represented a direct assault on American sovereignty and democracy, prompting a national reckoning with the vulnerability of the young republic. While the circumstances differed, the symbolism of an attack on the seat of government and the disruption of democratic processes resonated with the events of January 6, highlighting the enduring struggle to defend democracy against external and internal threats.

The insurrection at the Capitol prompted reflection on the fragility of democracy and the ongoing struggle to uphold democratic norms and principles in the face of challenges and threats. It served as a reminder of the importance of vigilance and resilience in defending the institutions and values that underpin American democracy while also raising questions about the root causes of political extremism and polarization.

After the insurrection, there was a renewed commitment to upholding the rule of law, promoting unity, and safeguarding democratic institutions against threats from within and without. The events of January 6 served as a sobering reminder of the enduring struggle to forge a perfect union and the imperative of collective action in preserving the promise of democracy for future generations.

International Reactions

The insurrection at the U.S. Capitol on January 6, 2021, triggered a wave of international reactions, reflecting the shock, condemnation, and concern felt by leaders and governments around the world. The unprecedented attack on the seat of American democracy prompted a global outpouring of solidarity with the American people and renewed scrutiny of the state of democracy in the United States.

Allies of the United States, including traditional partners in Europe and elsewhere, were quick to express solidarity with the American people and reaffirm their commitment to democratic values. Leaders from countries such as Canada, the United Kingdom, Germany, and France condemned the violence at the Capitol. They voiced support for the rule of law and the peaceful transition of power. Many emphasized the importance of upholding democratic norms and institutions amid political turmoil and unrest.

At the same time, adversaries of the United States seized on the events of January 6 as an opportunity to criticize American democracy and undermine confidence in democratic principles. Authoritarian regimes and governments hostile to the United States sought to exploit the unrest for propaganda purposes, portraying it as evidence of American hypocrisy and weakness. State-controlled media outlets in countries such as Russia, China, and Iran framed the insurrection as a sign of American decline and instability, seeking to sow doubt and division among the American people.

The global response to the insurrection underscored the interconnectedness of democracy and the shared responsibility to defend it against foreign and domestic threats. The attack on the Capitol served as a stark reminder of the fragility of democratic institutions and the importance of upholding democratic values in the face of challenges and adversity. It prompted renewed calls for solidarity and cooperation among democratic nations in promoting and protecting democracy worldwide.

In the aftermath of the insurrection, there was a recognition that the events at the Capitol had implications far beyond U.S. borders, shaping perceptions of American democracy and its role on the global stage. The international community looked to the United States for leadership and reaffirmation of its commitment to democratic principles while also reflecting on the need for collective action to address the root causes of political extremism and polarization that contributed to the attack on the Capitol.

Calls for Accountability

In the aftermath of the insurrection at the U.S. Capitol on January 6, 2021, there was a groundswell of calls for accountability from across the political spectrum and society. Lawmakers, activists, civil rights organizations, and ordinary citizens demanded thorough investigations, prosecutions, and accountability measures to ensure those responsible for inciting and participating in the violence were held accountable for their actions.

The attack on the Capitol was widely condemned as an assault on democracy and the rule of law. There was a consensus that those who had perpetrated violence and sought to undermine the peaceful transition of power must face the consequences of their actions. Calls for accountability encompassed a range of individuals and entities, including not only the rioters who had stormed the Capitol but also the political leaders and figures who had incited and encouraged them.

Lawmakers in Congress vowed to conduct investigations into the events of January 6 to uncover the full extent of the planning and coordination behind the attack and hold those responsible accountable. Congressional committees launched inquiries, held hearings, and issued subpoenas to gather evidence and testimony from witnesses, law enforcement officials, and other relevant parties.

In addition to congressional investigations, law enforcement agencies at the federal, state, and local levels launched criminal investigations into the insurrection, seeking to identify and prosecute individuals involved in the violence and destruction at the Capitol. Hundreds of arrests were made in the days and weeks following the attack, with charges ranging from trespassing and disorderly conduct to assault and conspiracy.

Pursuing justice was seen as essential in holding accountable those who had committed acts of violence and insurrection and sending a clear message that such behavior would not be tolerated in a democratic society. Accountability measures were crucial to restoring faith in democratic institutions and deterring future acts of political violence, thereby safeguarding the integrity of the electoral process and the peaceful transfer of power.

The calls for accountability after the insurrection reflected a commitment to upholding the rule of law and defending democratic principles against those seeking to undermine them. The pursuit of justice served as a reaffirmation of the resilience of American democracy and the determination of its citizens to protect and preserve it for future generations.

Long-Term Repercussions

The insurrection at the U.S. Capitol on January 6, 2021, left a lasting impact on American democracy and governance, prompting profound soul-searching and introspection about the state of the nation and the underlying causes of political polarization and extremism. The attack served as a stark reminder of the fragility of democratic institutions and the imperative of safeguarding the integrity of the electoral process.

The events of January 6 underscored the urgent need for reforms to strengthen democratic institutions and restore public trust in the political system. The breach of the Capitol exposed vulnerabilities in security protocols. It highlighted shortcomings in preparedness and response to acts of domestic terrorism and political violence. It prompted calls for comprehensive reviews and reforms to address systemic failures and prevent similar incidents from occurring in the future.

Moreover, the insurrection laid deep-seated divisions within American society and the corrosive effects of political polarization and extremism. The rhetoric of political leaders and the proliferation of disinformation and conspiracy theories fueled distrust, anger, and resentment among segments of the population, contributing to a toxic political climate characterized by hostility and division.

In the aftermath of the insurrection, there was a renewed sense of urgency to confront the root causes of polarization and extremism and bridge the widening divides in recent years. Efforts to promote dialogue, empathy, and understanding across political lines gained momentum, as did initiatives to combat disinformation and promote media literacy.

The events of January 6 also galvanized calls for accountability and justice for those responsible for inciting and participating in the violence. The pursuit of accountability was seen as essential not only to hold individuals accountable for their actions but also to reaffirm the rule of law and deter future acts of political violence.

Overall, the insurrection at the U.S. Capitol served as a wake-up call for the nation to confront the challenges facing its democracy and reaffirm its commitment to freedom, justice, and equality. It prompted a national reckoning with the state of American democracy and the imperative of protecting and preserving it for future generations. In the long term, the events of January 6 may catalyze positive change and renewal, inspiring efforts to strengthen democratic institutions, promote civic engagement, and foster a more inclusive and resilient democracy.

Unity and Healing

In the aftermath of the insurrection at the U.S. Capitol on January 6, 2021, there was widespread recognition of the urgent need for unity and healing to address the deep divisions that the attack had exposed. Political leaders, religious figures, and community organizers across the country issued calls for Americans to come together in the spirit of democracy and mutual respect, transcending partisan differences and ideological divides.

The events of January 6 shocked the nation. They laid bare the extent of political polarization and extremism that had taken root in American society. The attack on the Capitol was a stark reminder of the consequences of division and distrust, highlighting the importance of finding common ground and forging unity in the face of adversity.

Political leaders from both parties emphasized the importance of putting aside differences and working together to confront the nation's challenges. President Joe Biden, in particular, made unity a central theme of his inaugural address, calling for Americans to unite to heal the wounds of division and rebuild the fabric of democracy.

Religious leaders and faith communities were crucial in fostering unity and healing after the insurrection. Churches, mosques, synagogues, and other places of worship opened their doors to provide support and solace to those affected by the violence while offering messages of hope and reconciliation.

Community organizers and grassroots activists organized events and initiatives to promote dialogue, understanding, and empathy across political lines. They sought to create spaces for constructive engagement and mutual respect, fostering a sense of belonging and solidarity among diverse communities.

The pursuit of unity and healing was essential to address the immediate aftermath of the insurrection and lay the groundwork for long-term reconciliation and renewal. It was recognized that healing the wounds of division would require sustained efforts to build trust, foster empathy, and promote inclusivity in all aspects of society.

In the face of adversity, Americans rallied together to reaffirm their commitment to the principles of democracy and freedom. The pursuit of unity and healing served as a testament to the resilience of American democracy and the determination of its citizens to overcome challenges and build a better future for generations to come.

Impact on Democracy

The insurrection at the U.S. Capitol had a profound impact on American democracy, raising concerns about its health and resilience in the face of internal challenges. The attack served as a stark reminder of the fragility of democratic institutions and processes, exposing vulnerabilities that had been overlooked or underestimated.

One key concern the insurrection raised was the potential for political violence to disrupt the peaceful transfer of power, a cornerstone of democratic governance. The breach of the Capitol on January 6 threatened to undermine the legitimacy of the electoral process and erode public trust in democratic institutions. It raised questions about the readiness of law enforcement agencies and security protocols to respond effectively to acts of domestic terrorism and political violence.

Moreover, the insurrection highlighted the role of political leaders, media, and civil society in shaping the public discourse and influencing political behavior. The spread of disinformation, conspiracy theories, and inflammatory rhetoric in the months leading up to January 6 contributed to a toxic political climate characterized by division, distrust, and extremism. The attack underscored the need for greater accountability and responsibility among those in positions of power to uphold democratic norms and foster constructive dialogue.

In the aftermath of the insurrection, there was a renewed emphasis on the importance of civic engagement and active citizenship in safeguarding democracy. The attack served as a wake-up call for Americans to defend the values and principles that define their democratic system, including the rule of law, respect for human rights, and protection of minority rights. It prompted reflection on the responsibilities of individuals and communities to participate in the democratic process and hold elected officials accountable for their actions.

Overall, the impact of the insurrection on democracy was profound and far-reaching. It prompted soul-searching and introspection about the state of American democracy and the challenges it faces in the 21st century. The events of January 6 served as a reminder of the importance of upholding democratic norms and values, promoting civic engagement, and defending the integrity of the electoral process against threats from within and abroad.

Security Review and Reforms

In the wake of the insurrection at the U.S. Capitol, there was widespread recognition of the need for a comprehensive review of Capitol security protocols and procedures to prevent similar incidents from occurring in the future. Lawmakers, security experts, and government officials called for reforms aimed at bolstering the effectiveness of security measures while maintaining the openness and accessibility of the Capitol complex.

One of the primary areas of focus for security review and reforms was the Capitol Police force itself. There were concerns about the readiness and response capabilities of the Capitol Police in the face of a violent and coordinated attack. Questions about training, staffing levels, intelligence-gathering capabilities, and coordination with other law enforcement agencies were raised. As a result, there were calls for increased funding, resources, and training for the Capitol Police to ensure they were adequately prepared to respond to future threats.

Additionally, there was an emphasis on enhancing intelligence-sharing among law enforcement agencies to identify better and mitigate potential security risks. The insurrection exposed gaps in communication and coordination between federal, state, and local law enforcement agencies and intelligence agencies. Reforms were proposed to improve information sharing and collaboration to monitor and respond to emerging threats more effectively.

Physical security measures at the Capitol complex were scrutinized after the insurrection. Despite being one of the most heavily fortified buildings in the country, the Capitol was breached with relative ease by the mob on January 6. There were calls for perimeter security enhancements, such as installing additional fencing, barriers, and surveillance equipment, to better protect the Capitol from unauthorized access and potential acts of violence.

Furthermore, there was a recognition of the need to balance security and accessibility at the Capitol complex. While it was essential to safeguard the seat of American democracy, it was equally important to preserve the traditions of openness and public access that are integral to the democratic process. Efforts were made to implement security measures that would deter acts of violence and extremism without impeding the ability of the public to visit and engage with their elected representatives.

Overall, the security review and reforms undertaken in the aftermath of the insurrection aimed to strengthen the security posture of the Capitol complex while upholding the principles of democracy and transparency. By addressing vulnerabilities, improving coordination, and enhancing physical security measures, lawmakers sought to ensure that the Capitol remained a safe and secure environment for conducting government business and serving the American people.

Challenges to Electoral Integrity

The insurrection at the U.S. Capitol heightened existing concerns about the integrity of the electoral process. It highlighted the dangers posed by the spread of disinformation and conspiracy theories. The attack was fueled by baseless claims of election fraud and a refusal to accept the outcome of the 2020 presidential election despite multiple audits, recounts, and court rulings confirming the legitimacy of the results. This refusal to acknowledge the election results contributed to a climate of mistrust and division, ultimately culminating in the violent assault on the Capitol.

The events of January 6 underscored the importance of combating disinformation and protecting the integrity of elections to safeguard democracy. Efforts to undermine public confidence in the electoral process through false claims of fraud pose a significant threat to the democratic system, eroding trust in democratic institutions and undermining the legitimacy of elected leaders.

In response to these challenges, lawmakers, election officials, and advocacy groups mobilized to strengthen electoral integrity and restore public trust in the electoral process. This included measures to improve election security, enhance transparency in the voting process, and combat disinformation and foreign interference.

One key focus area was bolstering election security to protect against cyber threats and other forms of interference. This involved investing in cybersecurity measures to safeguard voter registration systems, voting machines, and election infrastructure from hacking and manipulation. Additionally, efforts were made to enhance auditing and verification procedures to ensure the accuracy and integrity of election results.

Another priority was enhancing transparency and accountability in the electoral process to build public trust. This included measures to improve voter education and outreach, expand access to voting information, and strengthen oversight of election administration. By promoting transparency and openness, election officials sought to reassure voters that their voices would be heard and their votes counted accurately.

Furthermore, there was a concerted effort to combat disinformation and misinformation campaigns to undermine confidence in the electoral process. This involved working with social media platforms, news organizations, and civil society groups to identify and counter false narratives and conspiracy theories. By promoting factual information and debunking falsehoods, stakeholders sought to empower voters to make informed decisions and resist efforts to sow doubt and discord.

Overall, the insurrection at the U.S. Capitol highlighted the urgent need to address challenges to electoral integrity and defend the democratic process against threats from within and abroad. Efforts to safeguard electoral integrity, combat disinformation, and promote transparency are essential to preserving the integrity of elections and upholding the principles of democracy.

Role of Leadership

During the insurrection at the U.S. Capitol on January 6, 2021, Trump's leadership role came under intense scrutiny and criticism. As the President of the United States at the time, Trump held a significant position of authority and responsibility for the safety and security of the nation. However, his actions and statements before, during, and after the events at the Capitol raised questions about his leadership and commitment to upholding democratic norms.

Before the insurrection, Trump had been promoting false claims of widespread voter fraud and disputing the outcome of the 2020 presidential election despite numerous courts and election officials affirming the legitimacy of the election results. In a speech delivered shortly before the Capitol breach, Trump urged his supporters to "fight like hell" and march to the Capitol to "stop the steal," using inflammatory rhetoric that many saw as incitement to violence.

As the chaos unfolded at the Capitol, with rioters breaching barricades, vandalizing property, and clashing with law enforcement officers, Trump initially hesitated to intervene or condemn the violence. Instead, he continued to make false claims about election fraud and tweeted messages sympathetic to the rioters, describing them as "patriots" and expressing understanding for their grievances.

Critics accused Trump of failing to fulfill his duty to protect the Capitol and uphold the rule of law, instead fanning the flames of unrest and emboldening those intent on subverting the democratic process. Lawmakers, including members of Trump's party, called for his immediate intervention to quell the violence and restore order. However, his initial response fell short of the decisive leadership expected in such a crisis.

After mounting pressure and calls for his resignation or removal from office, Trump eventually issued a video statement urging calm and calling for an end to the violence while still repeating false claims about the election. However, for many, this came too late and was perceived as too little to mitigate the damage caused by his earlier rhetoric and actions.

In the aftermath of the insurrection, Trump faced widespread condemnation and impeachment by the House of Representatives on charges of incitement of insurrection, making him the only president in U.S. history to be impeached twice. While the Senate ultimately acquitted him, the events of January 6 cast a shadow over his legacy. They raised serious questions about his fitness for leadership and commitment to the principles of democracy.

Resilience of Democracy

In the puzzle of American democracy, the resilience piece fits snugly into the bigger picture. Even when the insurrection at the Capitol sent shockwaves through the nation, democracy stood its ground like a sturdy piece of the puzzle, refusing to be shattered by adversity.

After the chaos subsided, lawmakers didn't relinquish their constitutional duty. They gathered once more to certify the Electoral College results, a crucial step in the democratic process. This act wasn't just about paperwork; it reaffirmed the principles that hold the nation together. It was a nod to the idea that no matter the challenge, the rule of law and the peaceful transition of power would prevail.

What stood out, though, was the united front leaders across the political spectrum presented. Democrats and Republicans, usually locked in fierce debates, found common ground in condemning the violence that shook the core of American democracy. This bipartisan show of solidarity wasn't just for show; it sent a powerful message that the nation's leaders were committed to protecting the democratic fabric that binds them all.

And then came the peaceful transfer of power, a moment that spoke volumes about the strength of democratic institutions. Despite the turmoil, the transition to the incoming administration happened smoothly, showcasing the enduring power of American democracy.

In the end, the aftermath of the insurrection revealed that American democracy, like a well-crafted puzzle, may face challenges and even moments of upheaval. However, its pieces fit together in a way that withstands the test of time. It's a testament to the system's resilience and the American people's unwavering commitment to the ideals of democracy and governance.

Fulfillment of Constitutional Duties

In the intricate puzzle of governance, fulfilling constitutional duties serves as one of the foundational pieces essential for the picture of democracy to come together. When chaos erupted on January 6, disrupting the solemn proceedings of certifying the Electoral College results, it seemed like a piece of the puzzle had been knocked out of place. Yet, true to the system's resilience, lawmakers didn't let the turbulence derail their commitment to upholding the Constitution.

Amid the echoes of violence, Congress reconvened with a sense of duty hanging heavy in the air. Despite the lingering shock and tension, they gathered to finalize the outcome of the 2020 presidential election. This wasn't merely a formality; it was a crucial step in reaffirming the democratic process and ensuring that the voices of millions of voters were heard and respected.

The disruption caused by the insurrection could have easily derailed the proceedings. However, Congress stood firm, unwavering in its dedication to upholding the rule of law. The Constitution served as their guiding light, reminding them of the sacred duty entrusted to them by the American people.

In the face of adversity, Congress's commitment to the peaceful transfer of power shone like a beacon of hope. Despite the challenges and disruptions, they remained steadfast in their resolve to ensure a smooth transition to the incoming administration, as mandated by the Constitution.

Fulfilling constitutional duties in the aftermath of January 6 wasn't just about ticking boxes on a checklist; it reaffirmed the fundamental principles upon which American democracy is built. It was a testament to the resilience of the system and a reminder that, even in the darkest of times, the beacon of democracy shines bright, guiding the nation forward on its path toward a perfect union.

Bipartisan Condemnation of Violence

In the intricate mosaic of American politics, bipartisan condemnation of violence is a rare but profound moment where the pieces align, transcending party lines for the nation's greater good. Following the unprecedented attack on the Capitol, leaders' swift and resolute response across the political spectrum was remarkable.

In the aftermath of the chaos that unfolded on January 6, Democrats and Republicans stood together, united in their denouncement of the violence and lawlessness that had transpired. It was a moment when political affiliations took a backseat to the shared commitment to democracy and the rule of law. Both sides of the aisle recognized the severity of the situation and the threat it posed to the very foundations of American governance.

The bipartisan condemnation of the insurrection wasn't merely a symbolic gesture but a rallying cry for accountability and justice. Leaders from both parties called for those responsible for inciting and perpetrating the violence to be held accountable for their actions. It was a clear message that no one is above the law in America, and attempts to undermine the democratic process will not be tolerated.

This united front sent a powerful message to the nation and the world that when defending the principles of democracy and upholding the sanctity of the electoral process, political differences fade into insignificance. It was a moment of solidarity and resolve, demonstrating that the spirit of bipartisanship can prevail even in the face of adversity.

The bipartisan condemnation of violence following the attack on the Capitol was a shining example of leadership in a time of crisis. It showcased the resilience of American democracy and served as a reminder that, ultimately, the values that unite us as a nation are more vital than any political divide.

Peaceful Transfer of Power

Despite the unprecedented circumstances surrounding the transition of power, the transfer of power from the outgoing administration to the incoming administration proceeded smoothly and peacefully. President-elect Joe Biden was inaugurated as the 46th President of the United States on January 20, 2021, in a ceremony that underscored the continuity and resilience of American democracy.

In the grand puzzle of governance, the peaceful transfer of power serves as a cornerstone piece, symbolizing the smooth transition from one administration to the next and demonstrating the enduring strength of American democracy. Despite the tumultuous events leading up to January 20, 2021, the nation witnessed a moment of continuity and resilience as President-elect Joe Biden took the oath of office to become the 46th President of the United States.

The inauguration ceremony itself was a testament to the enduring spirit of democracy. Against heightened security and lingering tensions, the peaceful power transfer unfolded with a sense of solemnity and purpose. It was a moment where the nation paused to reflect on its democratic traditions and reaffirm its commitment to the principles of governance.

As President Biden stood before the nation to take the oath of office, he not only assumed the responsibilities of the highest office in the land but also embodied the hopes and aspirations of millions of Americans. His inauguration marked a new chapter in American history, signaling a fresh start and a renewed optimism for the future.

But perhaps what was most remarkable about the peaceful transfer of power was not just the ceremony itself but the underlying message it conveyed. Despite the unprecedented circumstances and the challenges facing the nation, the institutions of American democracy remained steadfast and resilient. The transition from the outgoing administration to the incoming administration proceeded according to the principles in the Constitution, demonstrating that no individual or event is greater than the democratic ideals upon which the nation was founded.

In the end, the peaceful transfer of power was not just a ceremonial event but a reaffirmation of the fundamental principles that bind the nation together.

It was a reminder that, in the face of adversity, the institutions of democracy endure, ensuring that the governance puzzle remains intact for generations.

Commitment to Democratic Principles

In the intricate tapestry of American society, the commitment to democratic principles serves as the unifying thread that binds the nation together, even in times of uncertainty and upheaval. In the wake of the insurrection at the Capitol, the resilience of these principles was on full display as Americans from all walks of life reaffirmed their dedication to the ideals of democracy and governance.

Despite the shock and dismay caused by January 6, most citizens stood firm in rejecting violence and lawlessness. Instead of succumbing to chaos, they expressed grievances and sought change through peaceful dissent and democratic participation. It was a powerful statement that in America, the people's voice is heard not through acts of aggression but through the democratic processes enshrined in the Constitution.

The commitment to democratic principles was not merely a passive response to the events unfolding before them; it was an active reaffirmation of the values that define the nation. From community organizers to everyday citizens, Americans nationwide mobilized to defend democracy and uphold the rule of law. They took to the streets, engaged in civil discourse, and exercised their rights as citizens to demand accountability and transparency from their leaders.

At its core, the commitment to democratic principles is rooted in the belief that every voice matters and every vote counts. It is a recognition that the strength of a democracy lies not in its leaders alone but in the collective will of its people to strive for a more just and equitable society. And even in the face of adversity, Americans have repeatedly shown their unwavering dedication to these principles, ensuring that the flame of democracy continues to burn bright for generations to come.

Strength of Democratic Institutions

In the intricate mosaic of American governance, the strength of democratic institutions serves as the sturdy framework upon which the nation's democracy is built. Despite the unprecedented attack on the Capitol, these fundamental pillars of democracy—the judiciary, the legislative, and the executive—stood firm, a testament to their resilience and enduring importance.

The judiciary, entrusted with upholding the rule of law and ensuring justice for all, continued to fulfill its duties in the aftermath of January 6. Courts across the country remained open, dispensing justice and safeguarding the rights of individuals, even in the face of heightened tensions and security concerns. The independence and impartiality of the judiciary were reaffirmed, serving as a bulwark against attempts to undermine the rule of law.

Similarly, the legislative branch, comprising the Senate and the House of Representatives, continued to function despite the chaos that had unfolded within the halls of Congress. Lawmakers reconvened to carry out their constitutional duties, including certifying the Electoral College results and conducting oversight of the executive branch. The resilience of Congress in the face of adversity demonstrated its unwavering commitment to the democratic process and its role as a coequal branch of government.

Meanwhile, the executive branch, led by the President and the administration, remained steadfast in its responsibilities to govern the nation. Despite the transition of power occurring against a backdrop of heightened security measures and increased scrutiny, the peaceful transfer of power proceeded smoothly, underscoring the continuity and stability of American democracy.

The resilience of these democratic institutions in the aftermath of the attack on the Capitol was a testament to their durability and strength. Despite the challenges posed by external threats and internal discord, they remained steadfast in their commitment to upholding the principles of democracy and ensuring the peaceful functioning of government. In doing so, they reaffirmed their crucial role as the guardians of American democracy, capable of withstanding even the most formidable challenges.

Global Reverberations

In the interconnected web of global politics, the insurrection at the U.S. Capitol reverberated far beyond American shores, sparking reactions from leaders and citizens worldwide. The scenes of chaos and violence that unfolded in the heart of American democracy sent shockwaves through international communities, raising profound concerns about the stability of democratic institutions and the implications for global security and stability.

Nations worldwide watched with disbelief and alarm as the events of January 6 unfolded. The sight of rioters breaching the Capitol, the symbol of American democracy, shook the confidence of many in the resilience of democratic governance. Leaders from diverse corners of the globe expressed their concerns about the attack's implications for the United States and the broader international community.

The insurrection also prompted soul-searching among allies and adversaries alike about the credibility of the United States as a champion of democracy and human rights on the world stage. For decades, America has been a beacon of freedom and democracy, advocating for these principles in its foreign policy and diplomatic efforts. However, the images of violence and chaos at the Capitol raised questions about the nation's ability to uphold these ideals at home, casting doubt on its moral authority and leadership role in the world.

Moreover, the events of January 6 underscored the fragility of democracy itself, serving as a stark reminder that no nation is immune to the forces of division and extremism. In a world grappling with rising authoritarianism and populist movements, the attack on the Capitol served as a wake-up call to the urgent need to defend and strengthen democratic institutions everywhere.

In the aftermath of the insurrection, nations worldwide grappled with the attack's implications for their democracies and the global order. It served as a sobering reminder of the importance of safeguarding democratic principles and institutions at home and abroad to preserve peace, stability, and freedom for future generations.

Implications for National Security

In the intricate landscape of national security, the insurrection at the U.S. Capitol sent shockwaves through the corridors of power, revealing vulnerabilities in the country's ability to address threats from within its borders. The brazen attack exposed severe concerns about domestic extremism and the potential for political violence to undermine the nation's stability and security.

The events of January 6 laid bare the shortcomings in the government's capacity to anticipate and respond effectively to acts of domestic terrorism and political violence. Despite warnings and intelligence indicating potential unrest, the Capitol was overrun by a violent mob, catching law enforcement and security agencies off guard. The failure to adequately prepare for and quell the insurrection highlighted systemic weaknesses in the nation's security apparatus and prompted urgent calls for reform.

The attack also shed light on the growing threat posed by domestic extremism, fueled by ideological fervor and exacerbated by political polarization. The presence of extremist groups and individuals among the rioters underscored the need for a comprehensive strategy to combat radicalization and prevent acts of violence motivated by hate or extremist ideologies.

In the aftermath of the insurrection, there were widespread calls for reevaluating national security priorities and allocating resources to address emerging threats within the United States. Lawmakers and security experts called for increased investment in intelligence gathering, surveillance, and counterterrorism efforts focused on domestic extremism. They also emphasized strengthening partnerships between federal, state, and local law enforcement agencies to improve coordination and information sharing.

Furthermore, the attack prompted a broader conversation about the root causes of extremism and the role of political rhetoric in fueling radicalization. Many argued that divisive rhetoric and conspiracy theories propagated by political leaders had contributed to the climate of mistrust and hostility that culminated in the violence at the Capitol. Addressing these underlying factors would be essential to preventing future acts of domestic terrorism and safeguarding the nation's security.

In summary, the insurrection at the U.S. Capitol served as a wake-up call for policymakers and security officials, highlighting the urgent need to confront the rising threat of domestic extremism and strengthen the nation's defenses against acts of political violence. Only by addressing these challenges head-on and recommitting to the principles of democracy and the rule of law can the United States ensure the safety and security of its citizens in the face of evolving threats.

Healing and Reconciliation

In the aftermath of the tumultuous events at the U.S. Capitol, a collective call for healing and reconciliation echoed across the nation, seeking to mend the deep wounds inflicted by the attack and bridge the gaping divides that had been laid bare. Civil rights organizations, religious leaders, and community activists emerged as voices of reason and compassion, advocating for dialogue, empathy, and understanding to overcome the country's trauma and polarization.

At the heart of efforts to promote healing and reconciliation was the recognition of the need for empathy – the ability to understand and share the feelings of others. By fostering empathy, individuals could begin to see beyond their perspectives and experiences and recognize the humanity in those with whom they disagreed. This emphasis on empathy was essential in breaking down barriers and building bridges between individuals and communities torn apart by January 6.

Building trust was another crucial component of the healing process. In the wake of the insurrection, trust in institutions, leaders, and fellow citizens had been shaken. Restoring that trust required genuine efforts to rebuild relationships, demonstrate accountability, and uphold the values of transparency and integrity. Through these actions, trust could be rebuilt, laying the foundation for genuine reconciliation and collaboration.

Central to the pursuit of healing and reconciliation was the quest for common ground – areas of shared values, aspirations, and goals that could serve as the basis for unity and cooperation. Despite the deep divisions that had been exposed, there remained fundamental principles that most Americans could agree upon – a commitment to democracy, equality, and justice. By focusing on these shared values, efforts to promote healing and reconciliation sought to transcend partisan divides and foster a sense of unity and solidarity among Americans of all backgrounds and beliefs.

Ultimately, the journey toward healing and reconciliation would be long and arduous, requiring patience, persistence, and a commitment to dialogue and understanding. But by embracing empathy, building trust, and finding common ground, Americans could begin to heal the wounds of the past and forge a path toward a more united and inclusive future.

Defending Democracy

In the wake of the insurrection at the U.S. Capitol, a resounding call to action echoed across the nation, urging concerted efforts to defend democracy and fortify the institutions that uphold it. Civil society organizations, grassroots activists, and advocacy groups emerged as champions of change, mobilizing to advocate for reforms aimed at strengthening democratic governance, safeguarding civil liberties, and promoting civic engagement.

The events of January 6 served as a stark reminder of the fragility of democracy and the urgent need to protect it from foreign and domestic threats. Civil society organizations, long at the forefront of the fight for democracy, redoubled their efforts in the aftermath of the attack, working tirelessly to galvanize public support for reforms that would bolster democratic institutions and ensure their resilience in the face of adversity.

Grassroots activists, energized by the events at the Capitol, took to the streets and social media platforms to demand change. They organized protests, launched online campaigns, and mobilized their communities to advocate for policies that would safeguard the principles of democracy and protect the rights of all citizens. Amplified by urgency and determination, their voices were a powerful force for change in the fight against authoritarianism, extremism, and political violence.

At the heart of the movement to defend democracy was a commitment to accountability and transparency in governance. Advocacy groups pushed for reforms to strengthen oversight mechanisms, enhance electoral integrity, and combat corruption. They called for greater transparency in campaign finance, stricter regulations on lobbying, and measures to prevent foreign interference in elections – all aimed at safeguarding the integrity of the democratic process and restoring public trust in government institutions.

The insurrection at the Capitol served as a rallying cry for those committed to defending democracy against the forces of authoritarianism, extremism, and political violence. It galvanized a diverse coalition of individuals and organizations united in their belief in the fundamental principles of democracy – freedom, equality, and justice. Together, they stood as guardians of democracy, determined to protect and preserve the institutions that are the bedrock of American society.

Legacy for Future Generations

The events that unfolded on January 6, 2021, etched a profound legacy into the collective consciousness of future generations of Americans, leaving an indelible mark on their understanding of democracy, citizenship, and civic responsibility. The insurrection at the U.S. Capitol served as a cautionary tale, illuminating the dangers of extremism, the consequences of political polarization, and the fragile nature of democratic norms.

For future generations, the events of January 6 will serve as a stark reminder of the importance of safeguarding the principles upon which democracy rests. The attack on the Capitol exposed the vulnerabilities of democratic institutions to manipulation and exploitation by those who seek to undermine the rule of law and erode the foundations of democracy. It underscored the need for constant vigilance and active engagement in defending democratic values against internal and external threats.

Moreover, the events of January 6 highlighted the critical role of civic education in preparing citizens to participate meaningfully in the democratic process. It became clear that a well-informed and engaged citizenry is essential for the functioning of democracy. As such, there will be a renewed emphasis on teaching young Americans about the history of democracy, the rights and responsibilities of citizenship, and the importance of active participation in civic life. By instilling a sense of civic duty and fostering critical thinking skills, educators can empower future generations to become informed and engaged citizens capable of navigating the complexities of modern democracy.

Additionally, the insurrection underscored the importance of media literacy in an age of rampant disinformation and misinformation. Future generations will be tasked with distinguishing between fact and fiction, discerning reliable sources of information from propaganda and conspiracy theories. By equipping young Americans with the tools to evaluate information and analyze media content critically, educators can help mitigate the spread of falsehoods and ensure the integrity of public discourse in a democracy.

In summary, the legacy of January 6, 2021, will be one of reflection, resilience, and resolve. Future generations of Americans will inherit the responsibility of preserving and strengthening democracy for years. By learning from the lessons of the past and embracing the values of democracy, they can ensure that the events of January 6 serve not as a symbol of division and discord but as a catalyst for positive change and renewal in the ongoing pursuit of a perfect union.

Continued Investigations and Accountability

In the aftermath of the insurrection at the U.S. Capitol, a concerted effort was launched to uncover the truth behind the events of January 6 and hold those responsible accountable for their actions. This commitment to justice and accountability was driven by a collective determination to restore faith in democratic institutions and ensure such an attack could never happen again.

Law enforcement agencies, congressional committees, and independent commissions spearheaded ongoing investigations aimed at unraveling the full extent of the planning, coordination, and motivations behind the attack. These inquiries delved into various aspects of the insurrection, from the security failures that allowed the breach of the Capitol to the role of extremist groups and individuals in fomenting violence.

The investigations were conducted meticulously, gathering evidence, interviewing witnesses, and analyzing digital communications and social media posts to comprehensively understand the events leading up to and during the insurrection. Law enforcement agencies pursued criminal charges against those involved in the attack, from the rioters who stormed the Capitol to the individuals and groups suspected of inciting or organizing the violence.

Meanwhile, congressional committees held hearings and conducted oversight investigations to examine the systemic failures that contributed to the security breach and assess the response of government agencies and officials to the unfolding crisis. These inquiries aimed to identify lapses in intelligence-sharing, communication breakdowns, and other deficiencies in the government's preparedness and response efforts.

Additionally, independent commissions were established to provide impartial assessments of the events of January 6 and offer recommendations for preventing similar incidents. These commissions brought together experts from diverse fields to thoroughly examine the insurrection and propose reforms to strengthen democratic institutions, enhance security measures, and address the underlying causes of political polarization and extremism.

The pursuit of justice and accountability in the aftermath of the insurrection was not merely about punishing wrongdoers; it was about reaffirming the principles of democracy and upholding the rule of law. By holding those responsible for the attack accountable for their actions, society sent a clear message that acts of political violence and insurrection would not be tolerated in a democratic society.

Ultimately, the ongoing investigations into the events of January 6 served as a testament to the resilience of American democracy and the commitment of its citizens to defending the principles upon which it is founded. Through the pursuit of truth and justice, the nation took a crucial step toward healing the wounds inflicted by the insurrection and safeguarding the future of democracy for generations to come.

Lessons Learned

The insurrection at the U.S. Capitol triggered a period of deep reflection and introspection for the nation, prompting a soul-searching examination of the implications of the attack for its democracy and governance. In the aftermath of January 6, lawmakers, policymakers, and citizens alike engaged in a collective effort to draw lessons from the events and identify areas for improvement in the nation's security, political culture, and social cohesion.

One of the most significant lessons from the insurrection was confronting and addressing the nation's security infrastructure vulnerabilities. The breach of the Capitol exposed glaring deficiencies in the government's ability to anticipate and respond effectively to acts of political violence. It underscored the importance of bolstering security measures, improving intelligence-sharing mechanisms, and enhancing coordination among law enforcement agencies to prevent similar incidents in the future.

Moreover, the attack served as a stark reminder of the corrosive effects of political polarization and extremism on the fabric of American society. The deep divisions that fueled the violence at the Capitol highlighted the urgent need to bridge the ideological divide and foster greater civility and respect in political discourse. It prompted calls for a renewed commitment to dialogue, compromise, and bipartisanship as the cornerstone of a healthy democracy.

Additionally, the insurrection laid bare the nation's challenges in promoting social cohesion and inclusivity. The presence of extremist groups and individuals among the rioters underscored the persistent threat of racism, bigotry, and intolerance in American society. It prompted calls for more outstanding efforts to combat hate speech, promote diversity and inclusion, and address the root causes of radicalization and extremism.

Ultimately, the attack on the Capitol served as a wake-up call for the nation to reaffirm its commitment to democracy, justice, and equality. It prompted a collective recommitment to upholding the rule of law, defending democratic institutions, and safeguarding the rights and freedoms of all citizens. It reminded Americans of the fragility of democracy and the importance of remaining vigilant in the face of threats to its integrity and stability.

In the aftermath of January 6, the nation emerged more substantial and resilient, armed with valuable lessons learned from the events that shook the foundations of democracy. As the country moved forward, it did so with a renewed sense of purpose and determination to build a perfect union guided by the enduring values of freedom, equality, and justice.

The January 6, 2021, events at the U.S. Capitol marked a pivotal moment in American history, lasting and impacting democracy, security, and the rule of law. The insurrection served as a stark wake-up call to the urgent threats posed by political polarization, disinformation, and extremism while also revealing the resilience of democratic institutions and the unwavering determination of Americans to defend their democracy in the face of adversity.

The insurrection at the Capitol underscored the deep divisions and polarization that have increasingly characterized American politics in recent years. The attack was fueled by baseless conspiracy theories and false claims of election fraud, exacerbated by partisan rhetoric and inflammatory language from political leaders. It laid bare the dangers of political extremism and the consequences of demonizing opponents and sowing distrust in democratic institutions.

Moreover, the insurrection highlighted the pervasive influence of disinformation and misinformation in shaping public discourse and fueling political violence. Social media platforms and online echo chambers provided fertile ground for the spread of false narratives and conspiracy theories, contributing to a climate of distrust and hostility that culminated in the assault on the Capitol.

The events of January 6 also exposed critical vulnerabilities in security and preparedness at the highest levels of government. The breach of the Capitol raised serious questions about the adequacy of security measures and the ability of law enforcement agencies to respond effectively to emerging threats. It prompted a reassessment of security protocols and a renewed focus on protecting democratic institutions from future attacks.

Despite the shock and trauma of the insurrection, it also showcased the resilience of American democracy and the steadfast commitment of lawmakers, law enforcement officers, and ordinary citizens to uphold the rule of law and defend democratic norms. Members of Congress, staff, and law enforcement personnel exhibited remarkable courage and resolve in the face of violence, ensuring the continuity of government and the peaceful transition of power.

In the aftermath of the insurrection, there was a collective reckoning with the underlying factors that contributed to the attack and a renewed determination to address the root causes of political extremism and polarization. Efforts to strengthen democratic institutions, promote civic engagement, and combat disinformation gained newfound urgency, reflecting a commitment to safeguarding democracy and preserving the integrity of the electoral process.

In conclusion, the January 6 insurrection at the U.S. Capitol served as a sobering reminder of the fragility of democracy and the ongoing struggle to uphold democratic values in the face of evolving threats. It sparked a national conversation about the future of American democracy and the responsibilities of citizens and leaders alike in defending and preserving it for future generations.

LEGACY OF JANUARY 6

The legacy of January 6, 2021, is profound and far-reaching, leaving an indelible mark on American politics, society, and democracy. The events of that day served as a stark reminder of the fragility of democratic norms and the enduring challenges facing the nation. Several critical aspects of this legacy include

Shaping Public Discourse and Policy Debates

The insurrection at the U.S. Capitol in January 2021 marked a pivotal moment in American history, jolting the nation's collective conscience and igniting a cascade of repercussions that rippled through every facet of public life. This chapter delves into how the events of January 6 fundamentally reshaped the national conversation and policy debates in the United States, casting a stark light on pressing issues such as political extremism, disinformation, and the fragility of democratic norms.

The insurrection, fueled by baseless claims of election fraud and stoked by months of divisive rhetoric, thrust these critical challenges to the forefront of public discourse with an unparalleled urgency. As the world watched in disbelief, the storming of the Capitol laid bare the deep-seated divisions within American society. It underscored the dire consequences of unchecked polarization.

In the aftermath of this unprecedented attack on democracy, policymakers and the public were forced to confront the harsh realities of political extremism and its corrosive impact on the fabric of society. The insurrection served as a wake-up call, compelling leaders at all levels of government to reassess their approach to addressing the rise of radical ideologies and safeguarding democratic institutions.

Moreover, the events of January 6 exposed the pervasive influence of disinformation and misinformation in shaping public opinion and fomenting unrest. The spread of false narratives and conspiracy theories, amplified through social media and partisan news outlets, played a central role in fueling the anger and mistrust that culminated in violence at the Capitol. As a result, efforts to combat the spread of disinformation and promote media literacy emerged as urgent imperatives in the quest to restore faith in democratic governance.

Perhaps most significantly, the insurrection underscored the fragility of democratic norms and the need for steadfast commitment to upholding the rule of law. The brazen attempt to overturn a free and fair election served as a stark reminder that democracy is not a foregone conclusion but rather a perpetual work in progress, requiring constant vigilance and collective action to defend.

In the wake of this seismic event, the national conversation shifted dramatically, with discussions around political polarization, disinformation, and democratic resilience taking center stage. The insurrection catalyzed legislative action, policy reforms, and grassroots movements to address the underlying causes of social and political unrest.

As the nation grapples with the enduring legacy of January 6, the imperative to confront these pressing challenges head-on remains as urgent as ever. By reckoning with the lessons of the past and rededicating ourselves to the principles of democracy and unity, we can forge a path forward toward a more resilient and inclusive future for all Americans.

Exposing Fault Lines in American Society

The attack on the U.S. Capitol on January 6, 2021, served as a stark revelation of the profound divisions that permeate American society, laying bare fault lines that cut across lines of race, identity, and political ideology. This chapter explores how the events of that day exposed the deep-seated fissures within the nation, highlighting the challenges of confronting and reconciling these divisions in pursuit of unity and healing.

The sight of rioters breaching the Capitol's hallowed halls sent shockwaves through the country, serving as a visceral reminder of the fractures that have long plagued American society. Images of Confederate flags and symbols of hate juxtaposed against the backdrop of one of democracy's most sacred institutions underscored the extent to which these fault lines had become not only visible but dangerously entrenched.

The events of January 6 did not emerge in a vacuum. However, they represented the culmination of years of simmering tensions fueled by political polarization and social unrest. From debates over racial justice and systemic inequality to clashes over immigration and cultural identity, America found itself increasingly divided along ideological fault lines that seemed to grow deeper with each passing day.

Moreover, the attack on the Capitol laid bare the stark disparities in how these divisions manifest across different segments of society. For marginalized communities, particularly people of color and religious minorities, the insurrection served as a chilling reminder of the persistent threats posed by white supremacy and extremist ideologies. Meanwhile, for many disillusioned Americans who felt left behind by the political establishment, the events of January 6 represented a misguided attempt to reclaim a sense of agency in an increasingly polarized and unequal society.

In the aftermath of the attack, the nation grappled with the daunting task of reckoning with these divisions and charting a path toward reconciliation and healing. Calls for unity rang out across the political spectrum. However, the road to true reconciliation proved fraught with obstacles and uncertainties.

Addressing the root causes of division and distrust requires more than just rhetoric; it demands a sustained commitment to fostering understanding, empathy, and dialogue across lines of difference. It necessitates confronting uncomfortable truths about the legacy of systemic oppression and working tirelessly to dismantle the structures of inequality that perpetuate division and exclusion.

As the nation confronts the enduring legacy of January 6, the imperative to bridge these divides and forge a more inclusive and equitable society has never been clearer. By embracing the principles of empathy, tolerance, and mutual respect, Americans can begin to heal the wounds of the past and build a future grounded in unity and solidarity.

Prompting Soul-Searching and Introspection

In the wake of the insurrection at the U.S. Capitol on January 6, 2021, Americans found themselves grappling with a profound sense of disbelief and disillusionment. This chapter delves into the collective moment of soul-searching and introspection that followed the attack as individuals and institutions across the nation sought to make sense of the events and reckon with their implications for the future of democracy.

The assault on the Capitol served as a wake-up call, jolting Americans out of complacency and prompting a period of deep reflection on the state of the nation. For many, the sight of rioters storming the halls of Congress raised troubling questions about how such a brazen attack could occur in the world's oldest democracy. It forced a reckoning with the fragility of democratic norms and the vulnerabilities that threaten to undermine the very foundations of American governance.

In the aftermath of the insurrection, there was a palpable sense of urgency to understand the root causes of the violence and to confront the uncomfortable truths about the divisions that have long plagued American society. This period of introspection prompted individuals from all walks of life to examine their complicity in perpetuating polarization and consider what role they could play in fostering reconciliation and healing.

For some, this meant confronting the uncomfortable realities of privilege and power dynamics that perpetuate inequality and exclusion. It meant acknowledging how systemic racism, economic injustice, and political disenfranchisement have shaped the fabric of American society and committing to actively challenging those injustices.

For others, the period of introspection prompted a reevaluation of personal beliefs and values as they grappled with the implications of aligning themselves with extremist ideologies or engaging in rhetoric that fueled division and hostility. It prompted a soul-searching journey to confront the demons of intolerance and prejudice lurking within and chart a path toward greater empathy, understanding, and solidarity.

At the institutional level, the events of January 6 prompted a similar reckoning as organizations and institutions across the public and private sectors confronted their roles in perpetuating division and discord. It sparked conversations about the responsibility of media outlets, social media platforms, and political leaders to foster a more inclusive and respectful public discourse, one that prioritizes truth, accountability, and mutual respect.

Ultimately, the soul-searching and introspection that followed the insurrection catalyzed change, inspiring a renewed commitment to democracy, unity, and equality. It reminded Americans of the enduring power of collective action and solidarity in the face of adversity, and it laid the groundwork for a more inclusive and resilient democracy for generations to come.

Erosion of Trust in Democratic Institutions

The insurrection at the U.S. Capitol on January 6, 2021, sent shockwaves reverberating across the nation, shaking the very foundations of American democracy to their core. This chapter explores how the attack on the Capitol shattered the confidence of many Americans in the integrity and resilience of democratic institutions, casting doubt on the government's ability to safeguard the principles of liberty, justice, and equality.

The breach of the Capitol, the hallowed seat of American democracy, struck at the heart of the nation's collective identity, leaving a scar that would not quickly heal. For many, the sight of rioters rampaging through the halls of Congress raised troubling questions about the government's capacity to protect its citizens and uphold the rule of law in the face of brazen acts of insurrection.

The events of January 6 laid bare the vulnerabilities of democratic institutions in the face of concerted efforts to undermine their legitimacy and authority. The breach of the Capitol was not merely an attack on a building but a direct assault on the principles of democracy itself, a stark reminder of the fragility of the institutions that form the bedrock of American governance.

In the aftermath of the insurrection, the erosion of trust in democratic institutions emerged as a pressing concern, threatening to erode the very foundation of American democracy. The breach of the Capitol shattered the illusion of invincibility surrounding the country's political institutions, exposing their susceptibility to manipulation, corruption, and violence.

Moreover, the erosion of trust in democratic institutions posed a significant challenge to restoring faith in the system and rebuilding a sense of national unity and cohesion. In an era marked by deepening political polarization and social division, the loss of confidence in the ability of government institutions to serve the standard good further exacerbated existing tensions. It undermined efforts to forge consensus and cooperation.

Addressing the erosion of trust in democratic institutions requires more than just symbolic gestures or rhetorical flourishes; it demands concrete actions to strengthen accountability, transparency, and integrity within government. It necessitates a commitment to upholding the rule of law and defending the principles of democracy against all threats, foreign and domestic.

Ultimately, the events of January 6 served as a sobering wake-up call, forcing Americans to confront the stark realities of democratic governance in an age of uncertainty and upheaval. By reckoning with the challenges posed by the erosion of trust in democratic institutions, the nation can begin to chart a path toward renewal and revitalization, reaffirming its commitment to liberty, justice, and equality for all.

Rise of Political Polarization and Extremism

The January 6, 2021, events served as a stark reminder of the deep-seated divisions and polarization that have come to define American politics in the modern era. This chapter explores how the attack on the U.S. Capitol highlighted the growing threat of political extremism and the dangers of ideological polarization, underscoring the urgent need to bridge the partisan divide and cultivate greater civility and respect in political discourse.

The presence of extremist groups and individuals among the rioters who stormed the Capitol laid bare the disturbing reality of rising political extremism in America. From white supremacists to anti-government militias, the diverse array of extremist ideologies represented among the insurrectionists underscored the breadth and complexity of the threat facing the nation.

Moreover, the events of January 6 laid bare the extent to which ideological polarization has permeated every facet of American society, from the halls of Congress to the dinner table. The toxic combination of echo chambers, misinformation, and inflammatory rhetoric has fueled a vicious cycle of division and hostility, driving Americans further apart and eroding trust in democratic institutions.

The legacy of January 6 serves as a sobering reminder of the urgent need to bridge the partisan divide and foster greater civility and respect in political discourse. It is a call to action for leaders across the political spectrum to set aside partisan differences and work together to pursue common goals, putting the nation's interests above personal or party gain.

Efforts to combat political polarization and extremism must extend beyond policy and legislation; they must also encompass a cultural shift toward greater empathy, understanding, and mutual respect. This requires fostering meaningful dialogue and engagement across lines of difference, promoting media literacy and critical thinking skills, and holding accountable those who seek to exploit division and sow discord for their gain.

Ultimately, the events of January 6 serve as a wake-up call for Americans to confront the dangers of political extremism and polarization head-on. By embracing the principles of unity, civility, and respect, the nation can begin to heal the wounds of division and forge a path toward a more inclusive, equitable, and resilient democracy for future generations.

Calls for Accountability and Justice

In the aftermath of the insurrection at the U.S. Capitol on January 6, 2021, the nation rallied behind a collective call for accountability and justice in the face of unprecedented violence and chaos. This chapter delves into the widespread demands for accountability that reverberated across the country as law enforcement agencies, congressional committees, and independent commissions embarked on investigations to uncover the truth behind the events of that fateful day.

The brazen assault on the Capitol, orchestrated by a mob of rioters incited by baseless claims of election fraud, sent shockwaves through the nation and laid bare the fragility of American democracy. In response, a resounding chorus of voices demanded swift and decisive action to hold those responsible for the attack accountable for their actions.

Law enforcement agencies at the federal, state, and local levels launched comprehensive investigations into the events of January 6, working tirelessly to identify and apprehend the perpetrators of violence and vandalism. The pursuit of justice became a top priority, as law enforcement officials worked around the clock to bring the total weight of the law down on those who sought to undermine the rule of law and sow chaos in the heart of American democracy.

Law enforcement efforts, congressional committees, and independent commissions convened hearings and inquiries to uncover the root causes of the insurrection and identify systemic failures that may have contributed to its escalation. These were done to create preventative measures to let it happen again. Witnesses were called to testify, evidence was gathered and analyzed, and recommendations were made for reforms to prevent such a catastrophic event from occurring again.

Pursuing justice and accountability was essential to punish those responsible for the attack, restore faith in democratic institutions, and reaffirm the rule of law. By holding individuals and organizations accountable for their actions, the nation sent a powerful message that acts of violence and insurrection would not be tolerated and that those who seek to undermine democracy would be held to account for their crimes.

Ultimately, the calls for accountability and justice that followed the insurrection served as a testament to the resilience of American democracy and the unwavering commitment of the nation to uphold the principles of liberty, justice, and equality for all. By confronting the challenges posed by the events of January 6 head-on and holding those responsible accountable for their actions, the nation took a crucial step toward healing the wounds of division and reaffirming its commitment to a perfect union.

Efforts to Strengthen Democratic Resilience

The legacy of the insurrection at the U.S. Capitol on January 6, 2021, galvanized a wave of efforts aimed at fortifying the resilience of American democracy against future threats. This chapter explores the multifaceted initiatives launched after the attack to bolster security measures, enhance intelligence-sharing mechanisms, and promote civic education and media literacy as essential tools for safeguarding the integrity of democratic institutions.

In response to the unprecedented breach of the Capitol, lawmakers and policymakers swiftly proposed a series of reforms designed to shore up security measures and prevent similar incidents from occurring in the future. These efforts included bolstering physical security infrastructure, such as installing additional barriers and surveillance cameras, and implementing stricter protocols for access to sensitive areas of government buildings.

Moreover, there was a renewed emphasis on improving intelligence-sharing mechanisms and enhancing coordination among law enforcement agencies at the federal, state, and local levels. The events of January 6 revealed gaps in communication and coordination that escalated the attack unchecked, prompting calls for reforms to ensure more seamless cooperation and information-sharing among relevant stakeholders.

In addition to these security-focused initiatives, there were calls for more significant investment in civic education, media literacy, and critical thinking skills to equip citizens with the knowledge and tools they need to participate in democracy and resist efforts to undermine it actively. Recognizing the critical role of an informed and engaged citizenry in preserving the integrity of democratic governance - policymakers sought to expand access to high-quality civics education and promote media literacy programs in schools and communities nationwide.

By empowering individuals to evaluate information critically, discern fact from fiction, and engage thoughtfully in public discourse, these efforts aimed to inoculate society against the spread of misinformation and propaganda and foster a more resilient democracy capable of withstanding the challenges of the digital age.

Ultimately, the legacy of January 6 catalyzed change, inspiring a renewed commitment to strengthening the resilience of American democracy against internal and external threats. By investing in security measures, enhancing intelligence-sharing mechanisms, and promoting civic education and media literacy, the nation took proactive steps to safeguard the integrity of democratic institutions and uphold the principles of liberty, justice, and equality for all.

Erosion of Trust in Democratic Institutions

The insurrection at the U.S. Capitol on January 6, 2021, marked a profound rupture in the perception of invulnerability surrounding American democratic institutions. This chapter delves into how the breach of the Capitol, an iconic symbol of democracy, shattered the confidence of many Americans in the stability and integrity of their government, underscoring the vulnerability of democratic norms to manipulation and exploitation by those seeking to undermine the rule of law.

The siege on the Capitol was not just an attack on a building; it was an assault on the very foundations of American democracy. For generations, the

Capitol had stood as a beacon of liberty and a testament to the resilience of democratic governance. Its breach sent shockwaves through the nation, shaking the faith of many in the institutions that form the bedrock of American democracy.

The erosion of trust in democratic institutions was not sudden but the culmination of years of simmering discontent and political polarization. From allegations of voter fraud to conspiracy theories about deep state machinations, doubts about the integrity of the electoral process and the legitimacy of government institutions have been steadily gaining traction in the public consciousness.

The events of January 6 served as a wake-up call, laying bare the vulnerabilities of democratic norms to manipulation and exploitation by those with nefarious intent. The sight of rioters rampaging through the halls of Congress underscored the fragility of democratic institutions in the face of concerted efforts to undermine their legitimacy and authority.

Moreover, the erosion of trust in democratic institutions posed a grave threat to the very fabric of American society, fueling a sense of disillusionment and cynicism that eroded the bonds of civic engagement and solidarity. As faith in the political process waned, so did citizens' willingness to participate actively in democracy, deepening the divide between the governed and the governing.

Addressing the erosion of trust in democratic institutions requires more than just symbolic gestures or superficial reforms; it demands a concerted effort to rebuild confidence in the integrity and legitimacy of government. This requires transparency, accountability, and a commitment to upholding the rule of law, even in adversity.

Ultimately, the events of January 6 serve as a sobering reminder of the fragility of democratic norms and the constant vigilance required to safeguard them against threats from within and without. By confronting the challenges posed by the erosion of trust in democratic institutions head-on, the nation can rebuild faith in the promise of democracy and reaffirm its commitment to a more perfect union.

Heightened Awareness of Political Extremism and Polarization

The January 6, 2021, events cast a glaring spotlight on the alarming rise of political extremism and the widening chasm between ideological factions in American society. This chapter delves into how the presence of extremist groups and individuals among the rioters who stormed the U.S. Capitol underscored the dangers of radicalization and the potential for violence fueled by ideological fervor, prompting a renewed focus on addressing the root causes of polarization and fostering greater unity and understanding among Americans.

The sight of rioters, some brandishing symbols of hate and espousing extremist ideologies, laying siege to the seat of American democracy served as a chilling reminder of the grave threat posed by political extremism. From white supremacists to anti-government militias, the diverse array of extremist groups represented among the insurrectionists laid bare the depth and complexity of the challenge facing the nation.

Moreover, the events of January 6 brought into sharp relief the deepening divide between ideological factions in American society, fueled by a toxic combination of echo chambers, misinformation, and inflammatory rhetoric. The polarization of political discourse has become increasingly entrenched, creating fertile ground for radicalization and extremism to take root and flourish.

This heightened awareness of political extremism underscored the urgent need for concerted action to address the root causes of polarization and foster greater unity and understanding among Americans. It prompted soul-searching and introspection among individuals and institutions alike as the nation grappled with the uncomfortable truths about the divisions that have long plagued American society.

Efforts to combat political extremism and polarization must extend beyond mere rhetoric; they must encompass concrete actions to promote dialogue, empathy, and mutual respect across lines of difference. This requires investing in programs and initiatives that unite people to bridge divides, challenge stereotypes, and build bridges of understanding.

Ultimately, the events of January 6 served as a wake-up call, forcing Americans to confront the dangers of political extremism and polarization head-on. By embracing the principles of unity, civility, and respect, the nation can begin to heal the wounds of division and forge a path toward a more inclusive, equitable, and resilient democracy for future generations.

Calls for Accountability and Justice

Following the harrowing events of January 6, 2021, there arose an impassioned chorus of demands for accountability and justice to be served for those responsible for instigating and perpetrating the violence that shook the foundations of American democracy. This chapter explores the widespread calls for accountability that reverberated nationwide as law enforcement agencies, congressional committees, and independent commissions launched investigations to uncover the truth behind the insurrection and hold those accountable for their actions.

The breach of the U.S. Capitol, an iconic symbol of American democracy, sent shockwaves through the nation, prompting an immediate and persistent response from authorities and citizens alike. The brazen assault on the seat of government was viewed as an egregious affront to the rule of law and the principles of democracy, demanding swift and decisive action to ensure that justice was served and such an attack could never happen again.

In the aftermath of the insurrection, federal, state, and local law enforcement agencies launched exhaustive investigations to identify and apprehend those responsible for planning, inciting, and participating in the violence. A commitment to thoroughness and impartiality characterized these efforts, as authorities sought to uncover the truth behind the events of January 6 and hold all perpetrators accountable for their actions, regardless of their affiliations or motivations.

Simultaneously, congressional committees and independent commissions convened hearings and inquiries to comprehensively review the insurrection's circumstances and identify systemic failures that may have contributed to its escalation. Witnesses were called to testify, evidence was meticulously analyzed, and recommendations were made for reforms to prevent similar incidents.

Pursuing justice and accountability was essential to punish those responsible for the attack, restore faith in democratic institutions, and reaffirm the sanctity of the rule of law. By holding individuals and organizations accountable for their actions, the nation sent a powerful message that acts of violence and insurrection would not be tolerated and that those who seek to undermine democracy would be held to account for their crimes.

Ultimately, the calls for accountability and justice that followed the insurrection served as a testament to the nation's unwavering commitment to upholding the principles of liberty, justice, and equality for all. By confronting the challenges posed by the events of January 6 with resolve and determination, the nation took a crucial step toward healing the wounds of division and reaffirming its commitment to a more perfect union.

Renewed Commitment to Defending Democracy

In the wake of the insurrection at the U.S. Capitol on January 6, 2021, a groundswell of resolve and determination emerged among Americans to defend democracy and uphold the cherished principles upon which it was founded. This chapter delves into how, despite the challenges posed by the attack, citizens from all walks of life mobilized to condemn the violence and reaffirm their dedication to democratic values such as freedom, equality, and justice, serving as a powerful reaffirmation of the resilience of American democracy in the face of adversity.

The assault on the Capitol sent shockwaves through the nation, prompting a swift and resolute response from individuals and communities across the country. From elected officials to ordinary citizens, people from all corners of America united in a collective condemnation of the violence and a steadfast commitment to upholding the rule of law and democratic norms.

In the aftermath of the insurrection, citizens took to the streets, social media, and public forums to express their outrage and demand accountability for those responsible for the attack. Vigils were held, petitions circulated, and grassroots movements mobilized to call attention to the gravity of the situation and to reaffirm the fundamental values that underpin American democracy.

Moreover, the events of January 6 served as a rallying cry for civic engagement and political activism, inspiring a new generation of leaders and activists to step forward and take a stand in defense of democracy. From registering voters to running for office, individuals across the country seized the moment as an opportunity to make their voices heard and to play an active role in shaping the future of their communities and their country.

This collective response to the insurrection served as a powerful reaffirmation of the resilience of American democracy in the face of adversity. It demonstrated the enduring commitment of the American people to the principles of liberty, justice, and equality. It underscored the belief that democracy is not a static concept but a dynamic and ever-evolving process that requires active participation and vigilance.

Ultimately, the events of January 6 served as a stark reminder of the fragility of democracy and the constant vigilance required to defend it against threats from within and without. By coming together in solidarity and reaffirming their commitment to democratic values, Americans sent a powerful message that acts of violence and insurrection will not undermine the foundations of their democracy but rather strengthen their resolve to uphold them.

Erosion of Trust in Democratic Institutions

The breach of the U.S. Capitol on January 6, 2021, reverberated across the nation, shaking the very foundation of trust in American democratic institutions. This chapter explores how the unprecedented attack shattered the perception of stability and resilience that many Americans had taken for granted, revealing vulnerabilities in security protocols and raising profound questions about the ability of democratic institutions to withstand internal threats.

Before January 6, a sense of confidence and complacency existed regarding the strength and durability of American democratic institutions. The Capitol, the iconic seat of government, stood as a symbol of stability and continuity, its halls seen as holy and impervious to attack. However, the events of that fateful day shattered this perception, laying bare the stark reality of the vulnerabilities that lurked beneath the surface.

The breach of the Capitol exposed gaping holes in security protocols and failures in intelligence gathering and coordination, casting doubt on the government's ability to protect its citizens and uphold the rule of law in the face of brazen acts of insurrection. For many Americans, the sight of rioters rampaging through the halls of Congress was a wake-up call, forcing them to confront the uncomfortable truth that even the most hallowed institutions of democracy were not immune to attack.

In the aftermath of the insurrection, there was a palpable sense of disillusionment and skepticism among citizens as they grappled with the realization that the very foundation of their democracy had been shaken to its core. Confidence in the integrity and efficacy of democratic institutions was shattered, replaced by a sense of vulnerability and uncertainty about the future.

Moreover, the erosion of trust in democratic institutions posed a profound challenge to the fabric of American society, fueling a sense of cynicism and disengagement among citizens. As faith in the political process waned, so too did the willingness of individuals to participate actively in democracy, deepening the divide between the governed and the governing.

Addressing the erosion of trust in democratic institutions requires more than cosmetic reforms or symbolic gestures; it demands a concerted effort to rebuild confidence in the integrity and legitimacy of government. This necessitates transparency, accountability, and a commitment to upholding the rule of law, even in adversity.

Ultimately, the events of January 6 served as a sobering reminder of the fragility of democratic norms and the constant vigilance required to safeguard them against threats from within and without. By confronting the challenges posed by the erosion of trust in democratic institutions head-on, the nation can rebuild faith in the promise of democracy and reaffirm its commitment to a more perfect union.

Heightened Awareness of Political Extremism and Polarization

The January 6, 2021, events cast a glaring spotlight on the dangerous consequences of political extremism and polarization in American society. This chapter explores how the presence of extremist groups and individuals among the rioters who stormed the U.S. Capitol underscored the extent to which ideological divisions had become entrenched, serving as a wake-up call for a reevaluation of the factors driving polarization and the urgent need for more outstanding efforts to bridge the divide.

The assault on the Capitol laid bare the stark reality of political extremism and polarization in America as rioters, some waving flags of hate and espousing extremist ideologies, rampaged through the halls of Congress. It was a chilling reminder of the deep-seated divisions that have come to define American politics, fueled by a toxic combination of echo chambers, misinformation, and inflammatory rhetoric.

Moreover, the events of January 6 prompted a collective reevaluation of the factors driving polarization and extremism in American society. It forced a reckoning with the underlying grievances and grievances that fuel extremism, including economic inequality, social injustice, and political disenfranchisement. The insurrection served as a stark reminder that the consequences of ignoring these grievances are dire, with potentially catastrophic implications for the stability and cohesion of society as a whole.

The wake-up call provided by the insurrection underscored the urgent need for more extraordinary efforts to bridge the ideological divide and foster greater understanding and empathy among Americans. It highlighted the importance of promoting dialogue and engagement across lines of difference, challenging stereotypes, and building bridges of understanding to counter the corrosive effects of polarization and extremism.

Efforts to address the underlying grievances and grievances that fuel extremism must extend beyond mere rhetoric to encompass concrete actions aimed at addressing the root causes of inequality and injustice. This requires a commitment to tackling systemic issues such as economic inequality, racial discrimination, and political disenfranchisement through meaningful policy reforms and investments in social programs aimed at promoting equity and opportunity for all.

Ultimately, the events of January 6 served as a sobering reminder of the dangers of political extremism and polarization in American society. By confronting the underlying causes of division and working together to bridge the ideological divide, the nation can begin to heal the wounds of polarization and extremism and forge a path toward a more inclusive, equitable, and resilient democracy for future generations.

Calls for Accountability and Justice

In the aftermath of the insurrection at the U.S. Capitol on January 6, 2021, there was a resounding outcry for accountability and justice to be served for those responsible for the violence that shook the foundations of American democracy. This chapter delves into the widespread demands for accountability that echoed nationwide as law enforcement agencies, congressional committees, and independent commissions launched investigations to identify, prosecute, and prevent similar incidents in the future.

The brazen assault on the Capitol, orchestrated by a mob of rioters incited by baseless claims of election fraud, prompted an immediate and determined response from authorities and citizens alike. The unprecedented attack on the seat of government was viewed as an egregious affront to the rule of law and the principles of democracy, demanding swift and decisive action to ensure that justice was served and such an attack could never happen again.

In the wake of the insurrection, federal, state, and local law enforcement agencies launched extensive investigations to identify and apprehend those responsible for planning, inciting, and participating in the violence. A commitment to thoroughness and impartiality characterized these efforts, as authorities sought to uncover the truth behind the events of January 6 and hold all perpetrators accountable for their actions, regardless of their affiliations or motivations.

Simultaneously, congressional committees held hearings to examine the security failures that allowed the breach to occur and to assess the role of political leaders in inciting the violence. Witnesses were called to testify, evidence was meticulously analyzed, and recommendations were made for reforms to prevent similar incidents.

In addition to these efforts, independent commissions were established to conduct impartial inquiries into the events of January 6 and propose recommendations for preventing similar incidents. These commissions were tasked with conducting comprehensive reviews of the circumstances surrounding the insurrection, identifying systemic failures, and recommending reforms to strengthen the resilience of American democracy against internal threats.

Pursuing accountability was essential to punish those responsible for the attack, restore faith in democratic institutions, and uphold the rule of law. By holding individuals and organizations accountable for their actions, the nation sent a powerful message that acts of violence and insurrection would not be tolerated and that those who seek to undermine democracy would be held to account for their crimes.

Ultimately, the calls for accountability and justice that followed the insurrection served as a testament to the nation's unwavering commitment to upholding the principles of liberty, justice, and equality for all. By confronting the challenges posed by the events of January 6 with resolve and determination, the nation took a crucial step toward healing the wounds of division and reaffirming its commitment to a more perfect union.

Renewed Commitment to Defending Democracy

Despite the challenges posed by the insurrection at the U.S. Capitol on January 6, 2021, the events of that day ignited a renewed sense of unity and determination among Americans to defend democracy and uphold the values and principles upon which it is founded. This chapter explores how citizens from across the political spectrum came together to condemn the violence and reaffirm their commitment to democratic ideals, sparking a groundswell of support for efforts to strengthen democratic institutions, promote civic engagement, and protect the rights and freedoms of all citizens.

The assault on the Capitol sent shockwaves through the nation, but it also catalyzed unity and solidarity among Americans. Regardless of political affiliation, people from all walks came together to condemn the violence and defend democracy. From elected officials to ordinary citizens, there was a shared recognition of the need to safeguard the fundamental principles that underpin American democracy.

In the wake of the insurrection, there was a groundswell of support for efforts to strengthen democratic institutions and promote civic engagement. Citizens from across the country mobilized to defend the integrity of the electoral process, protect the rights of marginalized communities, and ensure that all voices were heard in the democratic process. It reaffirmed the belief that democracy is not a passive spectator sport but a participatory endeavor that requires active engagement and vigilance from all citizens.

Moreover, the insurrection served as a rallying cry for those dedicated to preserving the integrity of American democracy. It galvanized a new generation of leaders and activists to step forward and take a stand defending democratic values and principles. From organizing voter registration drives to advocating for reforms to strengthen democratic institutions, individuals across the country seized the moment as an opportunity to make their voices heard and to play an active role in shaping the future of their communities and their country.

The events of January 6 may have tested the resilience of American democracy. However, they also served as a powerful reminder of its enduring strength and resilience in adversity. By coming together in solidarity and reaffirming their commitment to democratic values, Americans sent a clear message that acts of violence and insurrection will not undermine the foundations of their democracy but rather strengthen their resolve to uphold them.

Ultimately, the insurrection served as a sobering reminder of the fragility of democracy and the constant vigilance required to defend it against threats from within and without. By renewing their commitment to defending democracy and upholding its values and principles, Americans can ensure that the events of January 6 do not define the nation's future but rather serve as a catalyst for positive change and a renewed dedication to building a more inclusive, equitable, and resilient democracy for future generations.

Reassessment of National Security Protocols

The insurrection at the U.S. Capitol on January 6, 2021, was a wake-up call that prompted a comprehensive reassessment of national security protocols and procedures. This chapter explores how the breach of the Capitol revealed critical weaknesses in intelligence gathering, communication among law enforcement agencies, and response coordination, leading to calls for reforms aimed at enhancing the government's ability to identify and mitigate threats to public safety, particularly those posed by domestic extremism. Strengthening national security emerged as a top priority to prevent similar incidents and protect the democratic process from future attacks.

The shocking events of January 6 laid bare the vulnerabilities in the nation's security apparatus as rioters breached the Capitol with alarming ease, causing chaos and destruction in their wake. The failure to anticipate and effectively respond to the attack exposed gaps in intelligence gathering, communication breakdowns among law enforcement agencies, and deficiencies in response coordination, highlighting systemic failures that allowed the insurrection to escalate unchecked.

In the aftermath of the insurrection, there was a collective recognition of the urgent need for reforms to bolster national security and protect the democratic process from future threats. Lawmakers, policymakers, and security experts alike called for a comprehensive review of existing protocols and procedures to identify shortcomings and implement targeted reforms to address them.

Key focus areas for reform included enhancing intelligence-gathering capabilities to identify and assess emerging threats, improving communication and information-sharing mechanisms among federal, state, and local law enforcement agencies, and strengthening response coordination to ensure a more unified and effective response to crises.

Moreover, there were calls for increased resources and funding to support efforts to combat domestic extremism and address the root causes of radicalization. This included investing in community-based initiatives aimed at preventing radicalization, promoting social cohesion, and countering extremist narratives that fuel violence and division.

Strengthening national security emerged as a bipartisan priority, transcending political divides as lawmakers and policymakers worked together to develop and implement reforms to safeguard the nation against internal and external threats. After recognizing the critical importance of a robust and resilient security infrastructure, efforts were made to prioritize the protection of democratic institutions and the safety of all citizens.

Ultimately, the reassessment of national security protocols prompted by the insurrection at the U.S. Capitol marked a pivotal moment in the nation's history, catalyzing a concerted effort to strengthen the government's ability to identify and mitigate threats to public safety and protect the democratic process from future attacks. By learning from the failures of January 6 and implementing targeted reforms, the nation took a crucial step toward ensuring that such a catastrophic event would never happen again, reaffirming its commitment to the principles of liberty, justice, and equality for all.

Impact on Global Perceptions of American Democracy

The events of January 6, 2021, had far-reaching implications for perceptions of American democracy on the global stage. This chapter explores how the sight of a violent mob storming the U.S. Capitol sent shockwaves around the world, undermining confidence in the United States' role as a global leader and advocate for democratic values. Allies expressed concern about the stability of American democracy. At the same time, adversaries seized on the unrest as evidence of systemic weakness and hypocrisy. Restoring America's reputation as a champion of democracy required a concerted effort to address the underlying issues that led to the insurrection and reaffirm the nation's commitment to democratic principles on the global stage.

The scenes of chaos and violence unfolding at the heart of American democracy reverberated across the globe, eliciting shock, disbelief, and concern among allies and adversaries alike. The breach of the Capitol, an iconic symbol of democracy, shattered the perception of American exceptionalism and raised serious doubts about the stability and resilience of the nation's political institutions.

For America's allies, the events of January 6 were deeply troubling, calling into question the United States' ability to serve as a reliable partner and defender of democratic values. Long viewed as a beacon of liberty and democracy, the United States suddenly appeared vulnerable and fragile, prompting allies to express concern about the future of American democracy and its implications for global stability.

Meanwhile, America's adversaries seized on the unrest as an opportunity to undermine confidence in the United States and advance their geopolitical agendas. From Moscow to Beijing, authoritarian regimes pointed to the chaos and division in America as evidence of the inherent weaknesses of liberal democracy, casting doubt on the viability of democratic governance as a model for other nations to emulate.

Restoring America's reputation as a champion of democracy required more than just words; it demanded concrete actions to address the underlying issues that led to the insurrection and reaffirm the nation's commitment to democratic principles on the global stage. This included holding those responsible for the attack accountable, strengthening democratic institutions, and promoting transparency, accountability, and the rule of law.

Moreover, it required a renewed commitment to dialogue, diplomacy, and cooperation with allies and partners worldwide to address common challenges and defend shared values. By demonstrating resilience, resolve, and a commitment to democratic principles, the United States could rebuild trust and confidence among its allies and adversaries, reaffirming its position as a leading voice for freedom, democracy, and human rights globally.

Ultimately, the impact of January 6 on global perceptions of American democracy underscored the fragility of democratic norms and the importance of safeguarding them against internal and external threats. By confronting the challenges posed by the insurrection with humility and determination, the United States could emerge more substantial and more resilient, reaffirming its commitment to the principles of liberty, justice, and equality for all, both at home and abroad.

Long-Term Impact on Political Discourse and Civic Engagement

January 6, 2021's legacy profoundly impacted the United States's political discourse and civic engagement. This chapter explores how the events of that day heightened tensions and deepened divisions within the electorate, making it increasingly difficult to find common ground and compromise on critical issues. However, they also sparked a wave of civic activism and engagement as Americans sought to reclaim their democracy and hold elected officials accountable for their actions. Grassroots movements and community organizing efforts flourished, signaling a renewed commitment to democratic participation and the pursuit of social justice.

The events of January 6 exacerbated existing divisions within American society, driving a wedge between political factions and making engaging in meaningful dialogue and debate increasingly challenging. The brazen assault on the Capitol served as a stark reminder of the deep-seated polarization and extremism that have come to characterize American politics, further eroding trust in institutions and exacerbating feelings of alienation and disenfranchisement among segments of the population.

However, amidst the chaos and uncertainty, a groundswell of civic activism and engagement emerged as Americans from all walks of life mobilized to reclaim their democracy and hold elected officials accountable for their actions. Grassroots movements and community organizing efforts flourished as individuals and groups came together to advocate for change, challenge systemic injustices, and demand accountability from those in power.

The events of January 6 catalyzed a renewed commitment to democratic participation and the pursuit of social justice. From organizing protests and rallies to volunteering for political campaigns and advocacy groups, Americans across the country seized the moment as an opportunity to make their voices heard and to play an active role in shaping the future of their communities and their country.

Moreover, the legacy of January 6 prompted a reevaluation of the importance of civic education and political engagement in fostering a healthy and vibrant democracy. Recognizing the need to equip citizens with the knowledge, skills, and resources to navigate the complexities of modern politics, there was a renewed emphasis on promoting civic literacy, critical thinking, and active citizenship from an early age.

Ultimately, the events of January 6 served as a sobering reminder of the fragility of democracy and the constant vigilance required to safeguard it against internal and external threats. By inspiring a new wave of civic activism and engagement, the legacy of January 6 signaled a renewed commitment to democratic participation and the pursuit of social justice, ensuring that the events of that day would not be in vain but rather serve as a catalyst for positive change and a more inclusive, equitable, and resilient democracy for future generations.

Challenges to Media Literacy and Information Integrity

The insurrection at the Capitol on January 6, 2021, brought to light the significant challenges posed by disinformation and misinformation in the modern information landscape. This chapter explores how false narratives and conspiracy theories spread rapidly on social media platforms, fueling anger and resentment among supporters of the outgoing administration and undermining trust in democratic institutions. It also delves into the raised concerns about the public's need to improve media literacy and critical thinking skills to discern fact from fiction and resist manipulation by malicious actors. Strengthening information integrity emerged as essential to safeguarding the democratic process and preserving the integrity of public discourse.

In the aftermath of the insurrection, it became increasingly clear that the proliferation of disinformation and misinformation played a central role in fomenting political violence and sowing discord within American society. False narratives and conspiracy theories spread like wildfire on social media platforms, exploiting echo chambers and algorithmic amplification to reach millions of users and fuel anger and resentment among supporters of the outgoing administration.

This rampant spread of falsehoods not only contributed to the escalation of tensions leading up to the insurrection but also undermined trust in democratic institutions and eroded confidence in the electoral process. It highlighted the public's susceptibility to manipulation by malicious actors and the urgent need to address the underlying factors driving the spread of misinformation.

One of the critical challenges identified after the insurrection was the need to improve media literacy and critical thinking skills among the public to discern fact from fiction and resist manipulation by nefarious actors. With the proliferation of digital media and the rise of social media platforms as primary sources of news and information, critically evaluating sources, verifying information, and differentiating between credible journalism and propaganda has become more critical than ever.

Efforts to strengthen media literacy and information integrity encompassed a range of initiatives, including educational programs in schools and communities aimed at promoting digital literacy and critical thinking skills, as well as media literacy campaigns to raise awareness about the dangers of misinformation and the importance of verifying information before sharing it.

Moreover, there were calls for greater transparency and accountability from social media companies and tech platforms to address the spread of disinformation and mitigate its harmful effects on public discourse. This included measures to combat the spread of false information, improve fact-checking processes, and promote responsible content moderation practices to curb the dissemination of harmful content.

Ultimately, the challenges posed by disinformation and misinformation in the wake of the insurrection underscored the need for a multifaceted approach to strengthening information integrity and promoting media literacy. By equipping the public with the knowledge, skills, and resources to navigate the complexities of the digital age, the nation can rebuild trust in democratic institutions and ensure that the democratic process remains resilient in the face of evolving threats.

Impact on Legislative Priorities and Governance

The insurrection at the U.S. Capitol on January 6, 2021, prompted a seismic shift in legislative priorities and governance in the aftermath of the attack. This chapter explores how lawmakers were compelled to prioritize measures aimed at strengthening democratic institutions, protecting the integrity of elections, and addressing the root causes of political extremism and polarization. It delves into the efforts to pass legislation to improve election security, combat disinformation, and promote transparency and accountability in government. The events of January 6 catalyzed bipartisan cooperation on national security, civil liberties, and the rule of law.

In the wake of the unprecedented attack on the Capitol, lawmakers from both sides of the aisle were united in their determination to strengthen democratic institutions and safeguard the integrity of the electoral process. The events of January 6 served as a wake-up call, compelling legislators to prioritize measures to address the systemic vulnerabilities that allowed the insurrection to occur and prevent similar incidents from happening in the future.

One of the key legislative priorities that emerged after the insurrection was the need to improve election security and combat efforts to undermine the integrity of the electoral process. Lawmakers introduced bipartisan legislation to strengthen voter protections, enhance cybersecurity measures, and modernize election infrastructure to safeguard against foreign interference and domestic threats.

Additionally, there was a concerted effort to address the spread of disinformation and misinformation that played a central role in fomenting political violence and undermining trust in democratic institutions. Lawmakers proposed measures to promote media literacy, combat online misinformation, and hold social media companies accountable for their role in amplifying false narratives and conspiracy theories.

Moreover, the events of January 6 catalyzed bipartisan cooperation on various issues related to national security, civil liberties, and the rule of law. Lawmakers came together to pass legislation aimed at strengthening the nation's response to domestic terrorism, protecting the rights of peaceful protesters, and ensuring accountability for those responsible for inciting violence and insurrection.

The insurrection also prompted a renewed focus on promoting transparency and accountability in government. Lawmakers introduced legislation to increase oversight of law enforcement agencies, enhance whistleblower protections, and promote greater transparency in government operations to rebuild public trust and confidence in democratic institutions.

Ultimately, the impact of the insurrection on legislative priorities and governance was profound, reshaping the political landscape and catalyzing bipartisan cooperation on issues of critical importance to the future of democracy. By prioritizing measures to strengthen democratic institutions, protect the integrity of elections, and address the root causes of political extremism and polarization, lawmakers demonstrated their commitment to upholding the principles of democracy and ensuring that the events of January 6 would not be in vain.

Consequences for Perpetrators and Enablers

The legacy of January 6, 2021, left a lasting imprint on those responsible for inciting, planning, and participating in the attack on the Capitol. This chapter explores how perpetrators faced legal repercussions, including arrests, prosecutions, and convictions for their actions, while elected officials and public figures who played a role in inciting the violence faced political consequences, including censure, impeachment, and loss of public trust. The accountability measures implemented after the insurrection were intended to send a clear message that the rule of law would be upheld and that those who seek to undermine democracy would be held accountable for their actions.

In the aftermath of the insurrection, law enforcement agencies launched a comprehensive investigation to identify and apprehend individuals responsible for planning, inciting, and participating in the attack on the Capitol. Perpetrators were swiftly identified through video footage, social media posts, and eyewitness accounts, leading to a wave of arrests, prosecutions, and convictions for offenses ranging from trespassing and vandalism to assault and sedition.

The legal repercussions for those involved in the insurrection were severe, with many facing lengthy prison sentences and hefty fines for their actions. The swift and decisive action taken by law enforcement sent a clear message that acts of violence and insurrection would not be tolerated and that those who seek to undermine democracy would be held accountable for their actions.

Moreover, elected officials and public figures who were found to have played a role in inciting violence faced political consequences for their actions. Several lawmakers who had perpetuated false claims of election fraud and encouraged supporters to "fight" to overturn the election results faced censure, impeachment, and loss of public trust. These accountability measures served as a reminder that public officials are not above the law and have a responsibility to uphold the principles of democracy and respect the rule of law.

The consequences for perpetrators and enablers of the insurrection were intended not only to punish those responsible for the attack on the Capitol but also to deter future acts of violence and insurrection and to reaffirm the nation's commitment to upholding the rule of law and preserving the integrity of its democratic institutions.

Ultimately, the legacy of January 6 involved holding individuals and entities accountable for their actions and ensuring that justice was served for those who sought to undermine democracy. By enforcing the rule of law and upholding democratic principles, the nation demonstrated its resilience in the face of adversity. It sent a powerful message that acts of violence and insurrection would not go unpunished.

Cultural Reckoning and National Identity

The January 6, 2021, events sparked a profound cultural reckoning and soul-searching about America's national identity and values. This chapter explores how the sight of the Capitol under siege shocked the nation's conscience and forced Americans to confront uncomfortable truths about the state of democracy and civil society. Questions about the meaning of patriotism, the nature of political dissent, and the boundaries of free speech became subjects of intense debate and reflection. The legacy of January 6 spurred a national conversation about the values that define America and the collective responsibility to uphold them in the face of adversity.

The sight of the U.S. Capitol, the symbol of American democracy, besieged by a violent mob on January 6, 2021, shook the nation to its core. It was a moment of reckoning, forcing Americans to confront uncomfortable truths about their democracy and civil society. The shocking images of chaos and destruction broadcast around the world prompted a collective soul-searching about America's national identity and values.

Central to this cultural reckoning was a reevaluation of the meaning of patriotism and the nature of political dissent. The events of January 6 raised fundamental questions about the boundaries of acceptable behavior in a democracy and the responsibilities of citizens to uphold the rule of law and respect democratic norms. What does it mean to love one's country? How do we reconcile the right to protest with the obligation to respect the institutions that form the bedrock of our democracy? These were among the problematic questions Americans grappled with in the aftermath of the insurrection.

Moreover, the events of January 6 sparked a heated debate about the role of free speech in a democratic society. While the First Amendment guarantees the right to freedom of expression, the insurrection raised concerns about the potential for speech to incite violence and undermine democratic values. Where do we draw the line between protected speech and dangerous rhetoric? How do we balance protecting democratic norms with the imperative to safeguard individual liberties? These questions became subjects of intense scrutiny and debate as Americans sought to reconcile the principles of democracy with the realities of political extremism and polarization.

The legacy of January 6 spurred a national conversation about the values that define America and the collective responsibility to uphold them in the face of adversity. It was a moment of introspection and self-examination as Americans grappled with the implications of the insurrection for the future of their democracy and the soul of their nation.

Ultimately, the events of January 6 served as a sobering reminder of the fragility of democracy and the constant vigilance required to defend it against internal and external threats. By engaging in honest dialogue about the challenges facing the nation and reaffirming their commitment to the principles of liberty, justice, and equality for all, Americans can begin to heal the wounds inflicted by the insurrection and forge a path toward a more inclusive, equitable, and resilient democracy for future generations.

Resilience and Hope for the Future

Despite the turmoil and division caused by the insurrection, the January 6, 2021, legacy embodied resilience and hope for the future. This chapter explores how the events of that day tested the strength of American democracy and the resolve of its citizens but also demonstrated the capacity for resilience and renewal in the face of adversity. The outpouring of support for democratic values, the peaceful transfer of power, and the commitment to building a more inclusive and equitable society offered glimmers of hope amid the darkness. The legacy of January 6, while complex and multifaceted, ultimately underscored the enduring strength of American democracy and the resilience of the American people in the face of profound challenges.

The insurrection at the U.S. Capitol on January 6, 2021, was a defining moment in American history, testing the resilience of the nation's democracy and the resolve of its citizens. However, glimmers of hope and resilience emerged amid unprecedented challenges, offering a path toward a brighter future.

One of the most striking demonstrations of resilience in the aftermath of the insurrection was the outpouring of support for democratic values and the rule of law. Despite the chaos and violence of January 6, Americans from all walks of life came together to condemn the attack on the Capitol and reaffirm their commitment to upholding the principles of democracy, freedom, and justice. This collective response served as a powerful reaffirmation of the nation's shared values and a rejection of efforts to undermine the foundations of American democracy.

Moreover, the peaceful transfer of power following the insurrection demonstrated the resilience of democratic institutions and the strength of the constitutional order. Despite the attempts to overturn the election results through violence and intimidation, the democratic process prevailed. President-elect Joe Biden was inaugurated as the 46th President of the United States in a ceremony marked by a spirit of unity and reconciliation.

The events of January 6 also sparked a renewed commitment to building a more inclusive and equitable society. In the wake of the insurrection, there was a growing recognition of the need to address the underlying grievances and inequalities that had fueled political extremism and polarization. From advancing racial justice and social equity to combating economic inequality and expanding access to education and opportunity, there was a sense of urgency to confront the nation's systemic challenges and forge a path toward a more just and equitable future for all Americans.

Ultimately, the legacy of January 6 underscored the enduring strength of American democracy and the resilience of the American people in the face of profound challenges. While the events of that day may have tested the nation's resolve, they also served as a powerful reminder of the resilience, hope, and determination that have defined the American spirit throughout history. As the nation confronted its darkest hour, it also found the strength and resilience to emerge more assertive, united, and committed than ever to the principles of liberty, justice, and equality for all.

Impact on Civil Liberties and Freedom of Expression

The insurrection at the U.S. Capitol raised significant concerns about the potential impact on civil liberties and freedom of expression. This chapter delves into how, while condemning the violence and extremism, there was also a recognition of the importance of safeguarding constitutional rights, including the right to protest and dissent. However, debates arose about where to draw the line between protected speech and incitement to violence, leading to discussions about regulating social media platforms and the responsibilities of tech companies in moderating harmful content. Balancing the preservation of civil liberties with the need to prevent violence and protect democratic institutions became a crucial challenge in the aftermath of January 6.

The January 6, 2021, events prompted a profound reckoning with the implications for civil liberties and freedom of expression in America. While the violent attack on the Capitol was universally condemned, there was also a recognition of the importance of safeguarding constitutional rights, including the right to protest and dissent.

However, the insurrection raised difficult questions about where to draw the line between protected speech and incitement to violence. The use of social media platforms to organize and coordinate the attack highlighted the role of online speech in fueling extremism and sowing discord within American society. As a result, there were growing calls for greater regulation of social media platforms and increased accountability for tech companies in moderating harmful content.

The debate over the regulation of social media platforms and the responsibilities of tech companies in moderating harmful content became a central focus in the aftermath of January 6. While there was a recognition of the need to prevent the spread of misinformation and incitement to violence, there were also concerns about the potential for censorship and infringement on free speech rights. Balancing the preservation of civil liberties with the imperative to prevent violence and protect democratic institutions emerged as a critical challenge for lawmakers and policymakers.

Moreover, the insurrection prompted a broader discussion about the erosion of trust in traditional media sources and the rise of alternative narratives and conspiracy theories. The proliferation of misinformation and disinformation online highlighted the public's need for greater media literacy and critical thinking skills to discern fact from fiction and resist manipulation by malicious actors.

Ultimately, the legacy of January 6 underscored the importance of safeguarding civil liberties and freedom of expression while acknowledging the need to address the spread of extremism and violence in society. By striking a balance between protecting constitutional rights and preventing harm to individuals and democratic institutions, policymakers sought to uphold the principles of democracy and ensure that the events of January 6 would not undermine the fundamental freedoms upon which America was founded.

Reconciliation and Healing

The legacy of January 6, 2021, encompassed efforts to promote reconciliation and healing in the aftermath of the trauma and division caused by the insurrection. This chapter explores how communities affected by the violence came together to support one another, engage in dialogue, and find common ground. Civil rights organizations, religious leaders, and community activists were crucial in fostering empathy, understanding, and reconciliation among Americans of different backgrounds and beliefs. These efforts sought to bridge the deep divisions exposed by the attack and promote healing and unity in the national discourse.

In the aftermath of the insurrection at the U.S. Capitol, there was a collective recognition of the need to promote reconciliation and healing in the wake of the trauma and division caused by the violence. Communities affected by the attack came together to support one another, engage in dialogue, and find common ground in adversity.

Civil rights organizations, religious leaders, and community activists were crucial in fostering empathy, understanding, and reconciliation among Americans of different backgrounds and beliefs. They organized healing circles, interfaith prayer services, and community forums to provide spaces for reflection, dialogue, and healing in the wake of the insurrection. These efforts sought to bridge the deep divisions that the attack had exposed and promote healing and unity in the national discourse.

Moreover, there were grassroots efforts to promote reconciliation and healing at the local level, with communities coming together to address the underlying grievances and inequalities that had fueled political extremism and polarization. From organizing neighborhood clean-up events to supporting local businesses impacted by the violence, Americans nationwide sought to demonstrate solidarity and support for one another in the aftermath of the insurrection.

At the national level, political leaders from both parties called for unity and healing in the wake of the insurrection. President Biden and Vice President Harris emphasized the importance of coming together to confront the country's challenges and build a more just and equitable future for all Americans. They called on Americans to reject the politics of division and to embrace the values of empathy, compassion, and unity that have long defined the nation's character.

Ultimately, the legacy of January 6 included a renewed commitment to promoting reconciliation and healing in the face of division and discord. By fostering empathy, understanding, and reconciliation among Americans of different backgrounds and beliefs, communities sought to heal the wounds inflicted by the insurrection and reaffirm their shared commitment to democracy, freedom, and justice for all.

Lessons Learned and Institutional Reforms

The events of January 6, 2021, sparked a critical period of introspection and lessons learned about the state of American democracy and the urgent need for institutional reforms. This chapter explores how lawmakers, policymakers, and experts examined the failures that allowed the insurrection to occur and proposed measures to strengthen democratic governance, enhance security protocols, and safeguard against future threats. Among the key initiatives undertaken were reforms to law enforcement practices, election security measures, congressional procedures, and efforts to address the underlying social, economic, and political factors driving extremism and polarization.

The insurrection at the U.S. Capitol on January 6, 2021, was a wake-up call for American democracy, prompting a profound reflection on its strengths and vulnerabilities. In the aftermath of the attack, there was a shared recognition among lawmakers, policymakers, and experts that systemic failures had allowed such a brazen assault on the heart of American democracy to occur.

One of the primary areas of focus in the aftermath of January 6 was reforming law enforcement practices to anticipate better and respond to threats to public safety and democratic institutions. Law enforcement agencies conducted thorough reviews of their handling of the insurrection, identifying shortcomings in intelligence gathering, communication, and response coordination. Efforts were made to improve training programs, enhance information-sharing mechanisms, and strengthen partnerships with other agencies and organizations to prevent similar incidents in the future.

Moreover, there was a concerted effort to bolster election security measures and safeguard the integrity of the electoral process against foreign interference and domestic threats. Lawmakers introduced legislation to enhance cybersecurity measures, modernize election infrastructure, and improve voter protections to ensure that every eligible American could exercise their right to vote safely and securely.

In addition to reforms to law enforcement practices and election security measures, there were also efforts to reform congressional procedures to enhance transparency, accountability, and effectiveness in governance. Lawmakers proposed changes to rules governing the certification of electoral votes, the conduct of congressional hearings, and the oversight of executive branch agencies to restore public trust and confidence in the legislative process.

Furthermore, there was a growing recognition of the need to address the underlying social, economic, and political factors driving extremism and polarization in American society. Efforts were made to invest in education, economic opportunity, and community development initiatives to promote social cohesion and resilience and to counteract the forces of division and discord that had contributed to the events of January 6.

Ultimately, the legacy of January 6 included a commitment to learning from past failures and implementing institutional reforms to strengthen American democracy and safeguard against future threats. By addressing the systemic vulnerabilities exposed by the insurrection and promoting transparency, accountability, and inclusivity in governance, lawmakers and policymakers sought to build a more resilient and responsive democratic system capable of withstanding the challenges of the 21st century.

Continued Vigilance and Preparedness

The January 6, 2021, legacy underscored the critical importance of continued vigilance and preparedness in defending democracy against internal and external threats. This chapter delves into how the attack served as a stark reminder that democracy is not guaranteed and must be actively defended by citizens and institutions alike. It prompted calls for ongoing monitoring of extremist movements, investment in intelligence gathering and analysis, and coordination among law enforcement agencies and other stakeholders to prevent future attacks on democratic institutions. The legacy of January 6 emphasized the need for constant vigilance in safeguarding the democratic process and protecting the rights and freedoms of all Americans.

The insurrection at the U.S. Capitol on January 6, 2021, left an indelible mark on the nation's collective consciousness, serving as a stark reminder of the fragility of democracy and the ever-present threat of extremism and political violence. In the aftermath of the attack, there was a heightened awareness of the need for continued vigilance and preparedness in defending democracy against internal and external threats.

The events of January 6 underscored the reality that democracy is not guaranteed and must be actively defended by citizens and institutions alike. The attack on the Capitol served as a wake-up call, prompting a renewed commitment among Americans to remain vigilant in the face of threats to democratic values and principles.

One critical lesson from January 6 was the importance of monitoring extremist movements and individuals who threaten democratic institutions. Law enforcement agencies, intelligence agencies, and other stakeholders redoubled their efforts to identify and assess potential threats, investing in intelligence gathering and analysis to stay ahead of emerging threats to public safety and national security.

Moreover, there was a renewed emphasis on coordination and collaboration among law enforcement agencies and other stakeholders to prevent future attacks on democratic institutions. Efforts were made to strengthen information-sharing mechanisms, improve coordination between federal, state, and local authorities, and enhance partnerships with community organizations and civil society groups to address the root causes of extremism and prevent radicalization.

The legacy of January 6 emphasized the need for constant vigilance in safeguarding the democratic process and protecting the rights and freedoms of all Americans. While the events of that day may have shaken the nation's confidence in its democratic institutions, they also served as a powerful reminder of the resilience and determination of the American people to defend their democracy against any threat, foreign or domestic. As the nation moved forward from January 6, it did so with a renewed sense of purpose and commitment to upholding the values of democracy, freedom, and justice for all.

Impact on Electoral Integrity and Voting Rights

The January 6, 2021, events heightened concerns about electoral integrity and voting rights in the United States. This chapter explores how the insurrection underscored the importance of safeguarding the electoral process against interference and ensuring all citizens have equal access to the ballot box. Efforts to enact voting rights legislation and strengthen election security measures gained momentum in the aftermath of the attack, as lawmakers and advocacy groups sought to protect the fundamental principles of democracy. The legacy of January 6 spurred renewed attention to issues such as voter suppression, gerrymandering, and campaign finance reform, focusing on promoting fairness, transparency, and inclusivity in the electoral system.

The insurrection at the U.S. Capitol on January 6, 2021, had profound implications for the integrity of the electoral process and the protection of voting rights in the United States. The attack was a stark reminder of safeguarding the electoral process against interference and ensuring all citizens have equal access to the ballot box.

In the aftermath of January 6, efforts to enact voting rights legislation and strengthen election security measures gained momentum as lawmakers and advocacy groups sought to protect the fundamental principles of democracy. There was a renewed sense of urgency to address the systemic vulnerabilities and threats to the electoral system exposed by the attack, including foreign interference, voter suppression, and disinformation campaigns.

One of the key initiatives undertaken in response to January 6 was the introduction of voting rights legislation aimed at expanding access to the ballot box and protecting voters' rights. Lawmakers proposed measures to restore key provisions of the Voting Rights Act, expand early voting and mail-in voting options, and combat efforts to suppress voter turnout through discriminatory voter ID laws and voter purges.

Moreover, there was a renewed focus on strengthening election security measures to safeguard against cyberattacks, disinformation campaigns, and other threats to the integrity of the electoral process. Lawmakers allocated funding for cybersecurity enhancements, modernization of election infrastructure, and increased transparency and accountability in the administration of elections to ensure that every vote was counted and every voice heard.

The legacy of January 6 spurred renewed attention to issues such as voter suppression, gerrymandering, and campaign finance reform, focusing on promoting fairness, transparency, and inclusivity in the electoral system. Lawmakers and advocacy groups worked together to address the root causes of electoral injustice and to promote reforms that would strengthen democracy and ensure that the electoral process remained free, fair, and accessible to all Americans.

Ultimately, the events of January 6 catalyzed action to protect electoral integrity and voting rights in the United States. By addressing systemic vulnerabilities and threats to the electoral system, lawmakers and advocates sought to uphold the principles of democracy and ensure that the voices of all Americans were heard in the democratic process.

Impact on Public Discourse and Trust in Media

The January 6, 2021, events also significantly impacted public discourse and trust in the media. This chapter delves into how the spread of misinformation and disinformation surrounding the attack highlighted the challenges of navigating a fragmented media landscape and discerning truth from falsehood. This led to calls for more outstanding media literacy education and efforts to combat the spread of false narratives online. The legacy of January 6 underscored the importance of responsible journalism, fact-checking, and critical thinking skills in preserving the integrity of public discourse and strengthening trust in democratic institutions.

The insurrection at the U.S. Capitol on January 6, 2021, not only shook the foundations of American democracy but also had a profound impact on public discourse and trust in the media. The spread of misinformation and disinformation surrounding the attack highlighted the challenges of navigating a fragmented media landscape and discerning truth from falsehood.

In the aftermath of January 6, there was a growing recognition of the need for more excellent media literacy education to help individuals critically evaluate information and distinguish between reliable sources and propaganda. Efforts were made to promote digital literacy skills and critical thinking abilities among the general public, focusing on empowering individuals to navigate the complexities of the modern media environment and identify misinformation and disinformation.

Moreover, there were calls for greater accountability and transparency in media reporting, emphasizing fact-checking and responsible journalism. Journalists and news organizations faced increased scrutiny in the wake of January 6, as the public demanded greater accuracy, objectivity, and integrity in reporting on matters of public importance.

Efforts were also made to combat the spread of false narratives and conspiracy theories online, with social media platforms implementing new policies and tools to identify and remove misinformation and disinformation. Tech companies invested in artificial intelligence and machine learning algorithms to detect and mitigate the spread of false content while promoting media literacy initiatives to help users critically evaluate online information.

The legacy of January 6 underscored the importance of responsible journalism, fact-checking, and critical thinking skills in preserving the integrity of public discourse and strengthening trust in democratic institutions. By promoting media literacy education and combating the spread of misinformation and disinformation, lawmakers, policymakers, and media organizations sought to empower individuals to make informed decisions and participate meaningfully in the democratic process.

Global Implications for Democracy and Human

Rights

Internationally, January 6, 2021, had far-reaching implications for democracy and human rights worldwide. This chapter explores how the attack on the U.S. Capitol sent shockwaves through global democratic movements, raising concerns about the fragility of democratic institutions and the rise of authoritarianism. It also sparked debates about the role of the United States in promoting democracy and human rights on the global stage, with some questioning the credibility of American leadership in light of the insurrection. The legacy of January 6 prompted reflection on the challenges facing democracies worldwide and the need for international cooperation to defend democratic values and norms.

The insurrection at the U.S. Capitol on January 6, 2021, reverberated around the world, casting a shadow over the global struggle for democracy and human rights. The brazen attack on one of the world's most iconic symbols of democracy sent shockwaves through global democratic movements, raising concerns about the fragility of democratic institutions and the rise of authoritarianism.

In the aftermath of January 6, there was widespread condemnation of the violence and a renewed commitment among democratic nations to defend the principles of democracy, the rule of law, and human rights. However, the attack also sparked debates about the role of the United States in promoting democracy and human rights on the global stage.

Some questioned the credibility of American leadership in light of the insurrection, highlighting the challenges facing democracies when the beacon of democracy itself came under attack. The events of January 6 served as a wake-up call for democracies worldwide, prompting reflection on the threats posed by extremism, populism, and authoritarianism to democratic values and norms.

Moreover, the legacy of January 6 underscored the importance of international cooperation in defending democracy and human rights. Worldwide, Democracies rallied together in solidarity, reaffirming their commitment to upholding democratic principles and supporting democratic movements in countries facing repression and tyranny.

Efforts were made to strengthen multilateral institutions and mechanisms for promoting democracy and human rights, focusing on fostering dialogue, cooperation, and solidarity among like-minded nations. The legacy of January 6 prompted a renewed sense of urgency in addressing the challenges facing democracies worldwide and the need for collective action to defend democratic values and norms in an increasingly uncertain and volatile world.

Ultimately, the events of January 6, 2021, served as a stark reminder of the fragility of democracy and the importance of safeguarding democratic institutions and human rights worldwide. By prompting reflection and action on a global scale, the legacy of January 6 underscored the shared responsibility of all nations to defend democracy and uphold the rights and freedoms of all people, regardless of borders or ideologies.

Long-Term Cultural and Psychological Impact

The January 6, 2021, legacy included a profound and long-term cultural and psychological impact on American society. This chapter explores how the trauma and upheaval caused by the insurrection left a lasting imprint on the collective consciousness, reshaping attitudes and perceptions about democracy, citizenship, and civic responsibility. The events of that day prompted individuals to confront uncomfortable truths about the nation's state and its role in shaping its future. This cultural reckoning spurred conversations about identity, belonging, and the meaning of American citizenship as citizens grappled with the attack's implications on their national identity and belonging.

The insurrection at the U.S. Capitol on January 6, 2021, had profound and far-reaching consequences for American society, leaving a lasting imprint on the cultural and psychological landscape of the nation. The trauma and upheaval caused by the attack shook the foundations of American democracy. They forced individuals to confront uncomfortable truths about the nation's state and its role in shaping its future.

In the aftermath of January 6, there was a collective reckoning with the implications of the attack on democracy, citizenship, and civic responsibility. Citizens grappled with questions about the fragility of democratic norms and institutions, the rise of political extremism, and the erosion of trust in government and fellow citizens.

The events of January 6 prompted individuals to reflect on their identities, values, and sense of belonging in a deeply divided and polarized society. There were conversations about the meaning of American citizenship and the responsibilities that come with it as citizens sought to reconcile their love for their country with the realities of its imperfections and challenges.

Moreover, the cultural and psychological impact of January 6 spurred conversations about the need for healing, reconciliation, and unity in American society. Communities came together to support one another, engage in dialogue, and find common ground in the face of adversity. There was a renewed sense of solidarity and purpose as individuals sought to rebuild trust, bridge divides, and work toward a more inclusive and equitable future.

The legacy of January 6 underscored the importance of confronting uncomfortable truths and grappling with the complexities of American identity and democracy. By sparking conversations about the meaning of citizenship, belonging, and civic responsibility, the events of that day prompted individuals to reevaluate their values and commitments and to strive toward a perfect union grounded in the principles of liberty, justice, and equality for all.

Impact on Law Enforcement and National Security Policies

The insurrection at the U.S. Capitol prompted a reassessment of law enforcement and national security policies to address the threat of domestic extremism. This chapter explores how the failure to prevent the attack exposed gaps in intelligence gathering, coordination among agencies, and response protocols. As a result, there were calls for reforms to enhance the government's ability to identify, monitor, and disrupt extremist groups and individuals. This included improving information sharing, increasing resources for counterterrorism efforts, and strengthening community partnerships to prevent radicalization and violence. The legacy of January 6 spurred a renewed focus on domestic security and the need to confront the root causes of extremism to safeguard against future attacks on democratic institutions.

The insurrection at the U.S. Capitol on January 6, 2021, served as a wake-up call for law enforcement and national security agencies, exposing critical vulnerabilities and shortcomings in their ability to address the threat of domestic extremism. The failure to prevent the attack exposed gaps in intelligence gathering, coordination among agencies, and response protocols, prompting a reassessment of law enforcement and national security policies.

In the aftermath of January 6, there were widespread calls for reforms to enhance the government's ability to identify, monitor, and disrupt extremist groups and individuals. Law enforcement agencies worked to improve information sharing and coordination efforts to ensure a more effective response to domestic threats. Additionally, there was increased focus on addressing the root causes of extremism and preventing radicalization through community engagement and outreach programs.

One key initiative undertaken in response to January 6 was allocating additional resources for counterterrorism efforts, including increased funding for intelligence gathering, surveillance, and investigative activities targeting domestic extremists. Lawmakers also proposed legislation to strengthen penalties for individuals involved in violent extremism and to enhance tools and authorities for law enforcement agencies to combat domestic terrorism.

Moreover, a renewed emphasis was on building community partnerships to prevent radicalization and violence. Law enforcement agencies worked closely with community leaders, religious institutions, and civil society organizations to identify and address potential threats, promote trust and cooperation, and empower communities to resist extremist ideologies.

The legacy of January 6 spurred a renewed focus on domestic security and the need to confront the root causes of extremism to safeguard against future attacks on democratic institutions. Implementing reforms to enhance information sharing, increase resources for counterterrorism efforts, and strengthen partnerships with communities, law enforcement, and national security agencies sought to prevent radicalization and violence and uphold the rule of law and democratic values.

Impact on Political Accountability and Transparency

The events of January 6, 2021, also profoundly impacted political accountability and transparency in the United States. This chapter explores how the attack on the U.S. Capitol led to demands for greater accountability from elected officials and public servants who were perceived to have contributed to the unrest or failed to uphold their oath of office. This prompted efforts to increase transparency in government, strengthen ethics and conflict-of-interest rules, and promote accountability measures such as independent oversight and whistleblower protections. The legacy of January 6 underscored the importance of holding leaders accountable for their actions and ensuring transparency and integrity in the democratic process.

The insurrection at the U.S. Capitol on January 6, 2021, not only shook the foundations of American democracy but also sparked a reckoning with political accountability and transparency. In the aftermath of the attack, there were widespread demands for greater accountability from elected officials and public servants perceived to have contributed to the unrest or failed to uphold their oath of office.

The events of January 6 prompted efforts to increase transparency in government and strengthen ethics and conflict-of-interest rules to prevent abuses of power and restore public trust. Lawmakers proposed legislation to enhance disclosure requirements for elected officials and public servants, including measures to require the disclosure of financial interests, lobbying activities, and potential conflicts of interest.

Moreover, there was a renewed focus on promoting accountability measures such as independent oversight and whistleblower protections to ensure that wrongdoing and misconduct could be reported and addressed without fear of retaliation. Efforts were made to strengthen oversight bodies' independence and effectiveness and empower whistleblowers to come forward with information about abuses of power and corruption.

The legacy of January 6 underscored the importance of holding leaders accountable for their actions and ensuring transparency and integrity in the democratic process. By promoting greater accountability and transparency in government, lawmakers and policymakers sought to rebuild public trust and confidence in democratic institutions and uphold the principles of accountability, integrity, and the rule of law.

Impact on Civic Education and Engagement

The January 6, 2021, legacy prompted a renewed focus on civic education and engagement as essential components of democracy. This chapter explores how the events of that day highlighted the importance of understanding democratic principles, institutions, and processes, as well as the responsibilities of citizenship. Efforts to promote civic education and engagement gained momentum, focusing on empowering individuals to participate in the democratic process, advocate for their rights, and hold elected officials accountable. The legacy of January 6 underscored the role of informed and engaged citizens in safeguarding democracy and shaping the nation's future.

The insurrection at the U.S. Capitol on January 6, 2021, served as a stark reminder of the fragility of democracy and the importance of an informed and engaged citizenry. In the aftermath of the attack, a renewed focus was on civic education and engagement as essential components of a healthy democracy.

The events of January 6 highlighted the importance of understanding democratic principles, institutions, and processes, as well as the responsibilities of citizenship. Citizens were reminded of their role in upholding the rule of law, holding elected officials accountable, and actively participating in the democratic process.

Efforts to promote civic education and engagement gained momentum in the wake of January 6, focusing on empowering individuals to become informed and active participants in their communities and the political process. Schools, universities, and community organizations launched initiatives to teach students and adults about the fundamentals of democracy, including the rights and responsibilities of citizenship, the importance of voting and civic participation, and the role of government in society.

Moreover, there was a renewed emphasis on providing resources and support for civic engagement activities, such as voter registration drives, community forums, and grassroots organizing efforts. Citizens were encouraged to advocate for their rights, voice their concerns, and work together to address pressing issues facing their communities and the nation.

The legacy of January 6 underscored the role of informed and engaged citizens in safeguarding democracy and shaping the nation's future. By promoting civic education and engagement, policymakers and community leaders sought to build a more resilient and inclusive democracy grounded in equality, justice, and active citizenship.

Impact on Interbranch Relations and Checks and Balances

The insurrection at the U.S. Capitol strained interbranch relations and tested the system of checks and balances in American governance. This chapter explores how the attack led to tensions between the executive, legislative, and judicial branches of government as each grappled with its role in responding to the crisis. This prompted discussions about the balance of power, the separation of powers, and the need for effective oversight and accountability mechanisms to prevent abuses of authority. The legacy of January 6 highlighted the importance of maintaining solid checks and balances to protect democracy from authoritarianism and ensure that no branch of government becomes too powerful.

The attack on the U.S. Capitol on January 6, 2021, not only threatened the physical security of the seat of American democracy but also strained interbranch relations and tested the system of checks and balances that underpins American governance. In the aftermath of the attack, tensions arose between the executive, legislative, and judicial branches of government as each grappled with its role in responding to the crisis.

The events of January 6 prompted discussions about the balance of power and the separation of powers enshrined in the U.S. Constitution. There were debates about each branch of government's appropriate roles and responsibilities in safeguarding democracy and upholding the rule of law. The executive branch faced scrutiny over handling security preparations leading up to the attack. In contrast, the legislative branch grappled with questions about its oversight and accountability mechanisms.

Moreover, the attack on the Capitol underscored the need for effective oversight and accountability mechanisms to prevent abuses of authority and ensure that no branch of government becomes too powerful. There were calls for increased transparency, accountability, and cooperation among the branches of government to restore public trust and confidence in democratic institutions.

The legacy of January 6 highlighted the importance of maintaining solid checks and balances to protect democracy from authoritarianism and ensure that no branch of government becomes too powerful. By reaffirming the principles of accountability, transparency, and the rule of law, policymakers and constitutional scholars sought to strengthen the foundations of American governance and safeguard democracy for future generations.

Impact on Social Cohesion and Community Resilience

The January 6, 2021, events profoundly impacted the United States' social cohesion and community resilience. This chapter explores how the attack on the U.S. Capitol deepened divisions within society, leading to increased polarization and mistrust among Americans. However, it also prompted communities to unite in solidarity, support, and resilience in adversity. Grassroots organizations, faith-based groups, and community leaders were crucial in fostering unity and healing, organizing events, discussions, and initiatives to promote understanding, empathy, and reconciliation. The legacy of January 6 highlighted the importance of building strong, inclusive communities capable of weathering crises and overcoming challenges through collective action and mutual support.

The attack on the U.S. Capitol on January 6, 2021, shook the foundations of American society and tested the resilience of communities across the nation. That day's events deepened societal divisions, exacerbating tensions and increasing American polarization and mistrust.

In the aftermath of January 6, communities grappled with the fallout from the attack. They sought to come together in solidarity, support, and resilience. Grassroots organizations, faith-based groups, and community leaders were crucial in fostering unity and healing, organizing events, discussions, and initiatives to promote understanding, empathy, and reconciliation.

Despite the challenges posed by increased polarization and mistrust, communities nationwide rallied together to support one another and reaffirm their shared values and aspirations. Individuals from diverse backgrounds and perspectives united in denouncing violence, upholding democracy, and working toward a more just and equitable society.

The legacy of January 6 highlighted the importance of building strong, inclusive communities capable of weathering crises and overcoming challenges through collective action and mutual support. By fostering unity, empathy, and resilience, communities sought to heal the wounds inflicted by the attack on the Capitol and reaffirm their commitment to democracy, equality, and justice.

Impact on Democratic Norms and Values

The January 6, 2021, legacy raised questions about the resilience of democratic norms and values in the United States. This chapter explores how the attack on the U.S. Capitol tested fundamental principles such as the rule of law, respect for electoral outcomes, and peaceful power transfer. While the democratic process ultimately prevailed, the events of that day exposed vulnerabilities and weaknesses that required careful attention and reinforcement. Efforts to defend and strengthen democratic norms and values gained momentum, focusing on promoting accountability, transparency, and integrity in governance. The legacy of January 6 underscored the importance of upholding democratic principles in the face of authoritarianism, extremism, and political violence.

The attack on the U.S. Capitol on January 6, 2021, represented a significant challenge to the democratic norms and values that underpin American society. The events of that day tested fundamental principles such as the rule of law, respect for electoral outcomes, and the peaceful transfer of power.

While the democratic process ultimately prevailed, the events of January 6 exposed vulnerabilities and weaknesses in the American political system that required careful attention and reinforcement. The attack raised questions about the resilience of democratic institutions and the ability of democratic norms and values to withstand external threats and internal divisions.

In the aftermath of January 6, efforts to defend and strengthen democratic norms and values gained momentum, focusing on promoting accountability, transparency, and integrity in governance. Lawmakers, policymakers, and civil society organizations worked to identify and address the root causes of political violence and extremism while also reaffirming the importance of upholding democratic principles in the face of authoritarianism, extremism, and political violence.

The legacy of January 6 underscored the importance of upholding democratic norms and values as essential safeguards against tyranny and oppression. By defending these principles, Americans sought to ensure that the events of January 6 would not undermine the foundations of democracy or erode the rights and freedoms guaranteed by the Constitution.

Impact on International Relations and Diplomacy

Internationally, the January 6, 2021, events had significant implications for U.S. foreign policy and diplomacy. This chapter explores how the attack on the U.S. Capitol shook the confidence of America's allies and partners in its commitment to democratic values and leadership on the global stage. It also provided fodder for adversaries and authoritarian regimes to undermine confidence in democratic governance and sow discord among democratic nations. The legacy of January 6 prompted a reevaluation of U.S. foreign policy priorities, with a renewed emphasis on promoting democracy, human rights, and the rule of law in international relations. Efforts to rebuild trust and strengthen alliances gained urgency as the United States sought to reaffirm its role as a champion of democracy and defender of freedom worldwide.

The attack on the U.S. Capitol on January 6, 2021, sent shockwaves around the world and had far-reaching implications for U.S. foreign policy and diplomacy. The scenes of violence and chaos undermined America's image as a beacon of democracy. They raised doubts about its commitment to democratic values and leadership on the global stage.

America's allies and partners expressed concern about the stability of American democracy and the implications of the attack on the future of democratic governance. The events of January 6 also provided propaganda material for adversaries and authoritarian regimes seeking to undermine confidence in democratic institutions and sow discord among democratic nations.

In response to January 6, U.S. foreign policy priorities were reevaluated, emphasizing democracy, human rights, and the rule of law in international relations. Efforts to rebuild trust and strengthen alliances gained urgency as the United States sought to reaffirm its role as a champion of democracy and defender of freedom worldwide.

The legacy of January 6 underscored the importance of defending democratic values and norms in the face of authoritarian challenges and external threats. By reaffirming its commitment to democracy, human rights, and the rule of law, the United States sought to rebuild trust, strengthen alliances, and promote a more stable and secure world order.

Impact on Law and Order

The legacy of January 6, 2021, impacted perceptions of law and order in the United States. This chapter explores how the attack on the U.S. Capitol raised questions about the government's ability to maintain public safety and uphold the rule of law in the face of political unrest and violence. It also prompted debates about the role of law enforcement agencies and the military in responding to domestic threats and protecting democratic institutions. Efforts to restore confidence in law and order gained traction, focusing on strengthening accountability mechanisms, improving training and oversight, and promoting community policing and engagement. The legacy of January 6 underscored the importance of upholding the rule of law as a cornerstone of democracy and ensuring that justice is applied fairly and impartially to all.

The attack on the U.S. Capitol on January 6, 2021, cast a shadow over perceptions of law and order in the United States. The scenes of violence and chaos raised questions about the government's ability to maintain public safety and uphold the rule of law in the face of political unrest and extremism.

The events of January 6 prompted debates about the role of law enforcement agencies and the military in responding to domestic threats and protecting democratic institutions. There were concerns about the adequacy of security measures and the effectiveness of coordination among law enforcement agencies in preventing and responding to such incidents.

Efforts to restore confidence in law and order gained traction after January 6, focusing on strengthening accountability mechanisms, improving training and oversight, and promoting community policing and engagement. Lawmakers, policymakers, and law enforcement officials worked to address the root causes of political violence and extremism and to ensure that justice is applied fairly and impartially to all.

The legacy of January 6 underscored the importance of upholding the rule of law as a cornerstone of democracy and ensuring that justice is applied consistently and transparently. By reaffirming their commitment to justice and accountability, Americans sought to restore confidence in law and order and uphold the integrity of democratic institutions.

Impact on Legislative Processes and Congressional Functioning

The events of January 6, 2021, had significant implications for legislative processes and the functioning of the U.S. Congress. This chapter explores how the attack on the U.S. Capitol disrupted the certification of the Electoral College results and temporarily halted congressional proceedings. This highlighted vulnerabilities in congressional security protocols and raised questions about the resilience of legislative processes in the face of political unrest. Efforts to strengthen congressional security and continuity measures gained momentum, focusing on enhancing preparedness, coordination, and response capabilities. The legacy of January 6 underscored the importance of ensuring the uninterrupted functioning of democratic institutions and the ability of lawmakers to fulfill their constitutional duties without fear of violence or intimidation.

The attack on the U.S. Capitol on January 6, 2021, had a profound impact on legislative processes and the functioning of the U.S. Congress. The violent breach of the Capitol disrupted the certification of the Electoral College results. It temporarily halted congressional proceedings as lawmakers were forced to evacuate or shelter in place.

The events of January 6 highlighted vulnerabilities in congressional security protocols. They raised questions about the resilience of legislative processes in the face of political unrest. There were concerns about the adequacy of security measures and the effectiveness of coordination among law enforcement agencies in protecting lawmakers and maintaining the integrity of congressional proceedings.

Efforts to strengthen congressional security and continuity measures gained momentum after January 6, focusing on enhancing preparedness, coordination, and response capabilities. Lawmakers and congressional leaders worked to identify and address gaps in security protocols, improve communication and coordination among law enforcement agencies, and ensure the safety and security of Capitol personnel and visitors.

The legacy of January 6 underscored the importance of ensuring the uninterrupted functioning of democratic institutions and the ability of lawmakers to fulfill their constitutional duties without fear of violence or intimidation. By strengthening congressional security and continuity measures, Americans sought to safeguard the integrity of the legislative process and uphold the principles of democracy and the rule of law.

Impact on Public Perception of Political Leadership

January 6, 2021's legacy also profoundly impacted public perception of political leadership in the United States. This chapter explores how the attack on the U.S. Capitol eroded trust in elected officials and government institutions, as many Americans questioned the integrity and effectiveness of political leadership in responding to the crisis. This prompted calls for accountability and transparency from elected officials and demands for more significant accountability measures such as ethics reforms and campaign finance regulations. Efforts to rebuild public trust and confidence in political leadership gained urgency, with a focus on promoting integrity, accountability, and ethical governance. The legacy of January 6 underscored the importance of leadership that is responsive to the needs and aspirations of the American people and committed to upholding the principles of democracy and the rule of law.

The attack on the U.S. Capitol on January 6, 2021, shook the foundations of public trust in political leadership in the United States. The scenes of violence and chaos eroded confidence in elected officials and government institutions, as many Americans questioned the integrity and effectiveness of political leadership in responding to the crisis.

The events of January 6 prompted widespread calls for accountability and transparency from elected officials. There were demands for more significant accountability measures, including ethics reforms and campaign finance regulations, to ensure that elected leaders were held to the highest standards of integrity and ethical conduct.

Efforts to rebuild public trust and confidence in political leadership gained urgency in the aftermath of January 6. Lawmakers and government officials worked to address the concerns of the American people and demonstrate their commitment to upholding the principles of democracy and the rule of law. This included promoting integrity, accountability, and ethical governance in all aspects of government.

The legacy of January 6 underscored the importance of leadership responsive to the needs and aspirations of the American people. By rebuilding public trust and confidence in political leadership, Americans sought to reaffirm their commitment to democratic values and ensure that government remains accountable to the people it serves.

Impact on Civic Activism and Grassroots Mobilization

The January 6, 2021, events sparked a wave of civic activism and grassroots mobilization in the United States. This chapter explores how the attack on the U.S. Capitol galvanized citizens from all walks of life to take action to defend democracy and uphold the rule of law. Grassroots organizations, advocacy groups, and community activists were crucial in mobilizing support for accountability measures, promoting voter participation, and advocating for reforms to strengthen democratic governance. Efforts to empower citizens to engage in civic activism and advocacy gained momentum, focusing on promoting inclusivity, diversity, and grassroots leadership. The legacy of January 6 underscored the power of ordinary citizens to effect positive change and hold elected officials accountable to the people's will.

The attack on the U.S. Capitol on January 6, 2021, served as a wake-up call for many Americans, galvanizing them into action to defend democracy and uphold the rule of law. In the aftermath of the insurrection, citizens from all walks of life came together to take a stand against political violence and extremism.

Grassroots organizations, advocacy groups, and community activists were crucial in mobilizing support for accountability measures in the wake of January 6. They organized rallies, protests, and campaigns to demand justice for those responsible for inciting and perpetrating the violence. Grassroots leaders also worked to promote voter participation and civic engagement, recognizing the importance of active citizenship in safeguarding democracy.

Efforts to empower citizens to engage in civic activism and advocacy gained momentum following January 6. Grassroots organizations focused on promoting inclusivity, diversity, and grassroots leadership, ensuring that all voices were heard in the fight for democracy. They provided resources, training, and support to individuals and communities looking to make a difference in their neighborhoods and beyond.

The legacy of January 6 underscored the power of ordinary citizens to effect positive change and hold elected officials accountable to the people's will. By harnessing the collective strength of grassroots mobilization, Americans sought to reclaim their democracy and ensure that the events of January 6 would not define the nation's future.

Impact on National Identity and Collective Memory

The legacy of January 6, 2021, also had a lasting impact on national identity and collective memory in the United States. This chapter explores how the attack on the U.S. Capitol challenged conventional narratives about American exceptionalism and democracy's invulnerability, prompting a reassessment of national identity and values. It led to debates about the meaning of patriotism, citizenship, and belonging in a diverse and divided society. Efforts to reconcile competing narratives and forge a shared national identity gained urgency, with a focus on promoting understanding, empathy, and unity. The legacy of January 6 underscored the importance of confronting brutal truths about the nation's past and present to build a more inclusive and equitable future for all Americans.

The attack on the U.S. Capitol on January 6, 2021, shook the foundation of American identity and challenged long-held beliefs about the strength and resilience of democracy. For many, the images of violence and chaos at the heart of American democracy shattered the myth of invulnerability, forcing a reckoning with the nation's history and values.

The events of January 6 prompted a reassessment of national identity and values, sparking debates about the meaning of patriotism, citizenship, and belonging in a diverse and divided society. Americans grappled with difficult questions about the state of their democracy and their place within it, confronting uncomfortable truths about systemic inequalities and injustices.

Efforts to reconcile competing narratives and forge a shared national identity gained urgency in the aftermath of January 6. Community leaders, educators, and activists worked to promote understanding, empathy, and unity among Americans of all backgrounds. They sought to build bridges across divides, fostering dialogue and collaboration in pursuit of a more inclusive and equitable society.

The legacy of January 6 underscored the importance of confronting brutal truths about the nation's past and present to build a more inclusive and equitable future for all Americans. By acknowledging the complexities of national identity and collective memory, Americans can work together to create a more resilient and cohesive society grounded in shared values of democracy, justice, and equality.

Impact on Social Media Regulation and Online Discourse

The January 6, 2021, events spurred a reevaluation of social media regulation and online discourse in the United States. This chapter delves into how the attack on the U.S. Capitol underscored the role of social media platforms in amplifying disinformation, facilitating extremist organizing, and inciting violence. It explores the subsequent calls for greater regulation of online speech and content moderation and efforts to hold tech companies accountable for their role in disseminating harmful content. The legacy of January 6 prompted discussions about the balance between free speech and public safety in the digital age, with a focus on promoting responsible online behavior and countering the spread of extremism and hate speech.

The January 6, 2021, events brought to light the significant influence of social media platforms in shaping public discourse and facilitating political organizing. Images and videos of the attack on the U.S. Capitol circulated rapidly on platforms such as Facebook, Twitter, and YouTube, amplifying disinformation and providing a platform for extremist groups to organize and incite violence.

In the aftermath of the attack, widespread calls were made for more significant social media platforms and online discourse regulation. Lawmakers and advocacy groups urged tech companies to take more aggressive action to combat the spread of disinformation and hate speech, including implementing more robust content moderation policies and removing accounts associated with extremist groups.

The legacy of January 6 prompted discussions about the balance between free speech and public safety in the digital age. While acknowledging the importance of protecting First Amendment rights, there was growing recognition of the need to address the harmful effects of online extremism and misinformation on democracy and public safety.

Efforts to hold tech companies accountable for their role in disseminating harmful content gained momentum, with calls for increased transparency, oversight, and regulation of social media platforms. This included proposals to revise Section 230 of the Communications Decency Act, which provides immunity to online platforms for content posted by their users.

The legacy of January 6 prompted a broader conversation about the responsibilities of tech companies in moderating online discourse and combating extremism. It underscored the need for collaborative efforts between government, civil society, and the private sector to address the complex challenges posed by social media regulation and online extremism in the digital age.

Impact on Government Transparency and Accountability

The legacy of January 6, 2021, also had implications for government transparency and accountability in the United States. This chapter explores how the attack on the U.S. Capitol raised questions about the transparency of government decision-making processes and the accountability of elected officials and public servants. It delves into the efforts to enhance transparency measures, promote open government initiatives, and strengthen oversight mechanisms to ensure the public can access information about government activities and decisions. The legacy of January 6 underscored the importance of government transparency and accountability in upholding the trust and confidence of the American people in their democratic institutions.

The January 6, 2021, events prompted a reevaluation of government transparency and accountability in the United States. The attack on the U.S. Capitol raised concerns about the transparency of government decision-making processes, particularly concerning security protocols and response efforts.

In the aftermath of the attack, there were calls for more significant transparency measures to ensure the public can access information about government activities and decisions. This included efforts to improve the release of public records, expand access to government data, and promote open government initiatives to enhance transparency and accountability.

Efforts to strengthen oversight mechanisms also gained momentum after January 6. Congressional committees launched investigations into the security failures that allowed the breach of the Capitol to occur, as well as the role of elected officials in inciting or enabling the violence. These inquiries aimed to hold individuals and agencies accountable for their actions and ensure that similar incidents could be prevented.

The legacy of January 6 underscored the importance of government transparency and accountability in upholding the trust and confidence of the American people in their democratic institutions. It highlighted the need for more extraordinary transparency measures to promote openness, accountability, and trust in government, particularly in times of crisis or uncertainty.

Impact on Electoral Reform and Democratic Participation

The January 6, 2021, events prompted a reexamination of electoral reform and efforts to promote democratic participation in the United States. This chapter explores how the attack on the U.S. Capitol highlighted vulnerabilities in the electoral process, including barriers to voting, threats to election security, and challenges to the legitimacy of election outcomes. It delves into the calls for reforms to strengthen election integrity, expand access to the ballot box, and protect voters' rights. Efforts to promote democratic participation gained momentum, focusing on empowering marginalized communities, combating voter suppression, and promoting inclusive and equitable elections. The legacy of January 6 underscored the importance of safeguarding the right to vote as a cornerstone of democracy and ensuring that all citizens have equal access to participate in the democratic process.

The January 6, 2021, events prompted a reevaluation of electoral reform and efforts to promote democratic participation in the United States. The attack on the U.S. Capitol raised concerns about the integrity of the electoral process. It highlighted vulnerabilities that needed to be addressed to safeguard democracy.

One of the critical issues highlighted by the attack was barriers to voting and threats to election security. Efforts to suppress voter turnout and undermine confidence in the electoral process had become increasingly prevalent, particularly in marginalized communities. In response, there were calls for reforms to strengthen election integrity, expand access to the ballot box, and protect voters' rights.

Efforts to promote democratic participation gained momentum in the wake of January 6. Advocates pushed for measures to empower marginalized communities, combat voter suppression tactics, and promote inclusive and equitable elections. This included initiatives to expand early voting options, streamline voter registration processes, and improve access to polling places, particularly in underserved areas.

The legacy of January 6 underscored the importance of safeguarding the right to vote as a cornerstone of democracy. It emphasized the need for comprehensive electoral reforms to ensure that all citizens have equal access to participate in the democratic process and that election outcomes reflect the people's will. By addressing barriers to voting and promoting democratic participation, the United States can strengthen its democracy and uphold the principles of freedom, equality, and justice for all.

Impact on Historical Memory and Commemoration

The January 6, 2021, legacy had profound implications for historical memory and commemoration in the United States. This chapter explores how the attack on the U.S. Capitol prompted discussions about how to remember and commemorate the events of that day, as well as their significance in American history. Efforts to preserve the memory of January 6 and its lessons gained traction, with a focus on promoting education, remembrance, and reflection. The legacy of January 6 underscored the importance of confronting brutal truths about the nation's past and present to build a more just, inclusive, and equitable future for all Americans.

The events of January 6, 2021, not only shocked the nation but also prompted reflection on how to remember and commemorate the attack on the U.S. Capitol. As the country grappled with the significance of that day in American history, efforts to preserve its memory and lessons gained momentum.

One fundamental discussion emerged about remembering January 6 and its national implications. Some advocated for formal commemorations and memorials to honor the lives lost and the bravery of those who defended democracy. Others called for educational initiatives to ensure that future generations understand the events of that day and their impact on American democracy.

Efforts to preserve the memory of January 6 also focused on promoting reflection and dialogue about the underlying issues that contributed to the attack. This included discussions about political polarization, the spread of disinformation, and the erosion of trust in democratic institutions. By confronting these problematic truths, Americans hoped to build a more just, inclusive, and equitable future for all.

The legacy of January 6 underscored the importance of remembering and commemorating significant events in American history, even those that are painful or uncomfortable. The United States can work toward healing, reconciliation, and progress as a nation by acknowledging the past and its lessons.

Impact on Government Preparedness and Crisis

Response

The January 6, 2021, events served as a wake-up call for the United States, prompting a thorough reassessment of government preparedness and crisis response capabilities. This chapter delves into how the attack on the U.S. Capitol exposed weaknesses in emergency response protocols, communication systems, and coordination among agencies. It further explores the subsequent efforts to improve preparedness for future crises, including training exercises, simulations, and updates to response plans. The legacy of January 6 underscored the importance of effective crisis management and coordination among federal, state, and local authorities to ensure the safety and security of the public.

The attack on the U.S. Capitol on January 6, 2021, revealed significant deficiencies in the government's preparedness and crisis response mechanisms. The breach of one of the nation's most iconic symbols of democracy exposed previously overlooked or underestimated vulnerabilities.

One of the critical shortcomings highlighted by the events of January 6 was the lack of coordination among law enforcement agencies and other emergency responders. The response to the attack was disjointed and ineffective, with delays in deploying reinforcements and securing the Capitol complex. Communication breakdowns further exacerbated the situation, hindering efforts to coordinate a unified response.

In the aftermath of January 6, a concerted effort was made to address these deficiencies and improve government preparedness for future crises. This included conducting comprehensive reviews of response protocols, identifying areas for improvement, and implementing corrective measures. Training exercises and simulations were conducted to test the effectiveness of response plans and ensure that personnel were adequately prepared to handle emergencies.

Additionally, there was a renewed emphasis on interagency cooperation and information sharing to enhance situational awareness and response coordination. Federal, state, and local authorities worked to establish more transparent lines of communication and protocols for sharing intelligence and coordinating resources during emergencies.

The legacy of January 6 underscored the importance of effective crisis management and preparedness in safeguarding the nation's security and democratic institutions. It served as a sobering reminder of the need for constant vigilance and readiness to respond to foreign and domestic threats. By learning from the events of January 6 and implementing necessary reforms, the United States took critical steps toward strengthening its resilience and ensuring the safety and security of its citizens.

Impact on Public Discourse and Political Dialogue

January 6, 2021's legacy brought significant implications for public discourse and political dialogue in the United States. This chapter delves into how the attack on the U.S. Capitol intensified polarization and divisiveness in the national discourse, leading to increased hostility and distrust among political factions. It further explores the subsequent efforts to promote constructive dialogue and bridge partisan divides, focusing on fostering empathy, understanding, and mutual respect. The legacy of January 6 underscored the importance of civility, decency, and inclusivity in public discourse and political engagement.

The attack on the U.S. Capitol on January 6, 2021, exacerbated existing divisions within American society and intensified polarization in the national discourse. The violent breach of the Capitol by a mob of extremists shocked the nation and deepened the rifts between political factions.

In the aftermath of January 6, political discourse became increasingly hostile and contentious as partisans retreated further into their respective echo chambers and demonized their opponents. Trust in institutions and the media eroded as conspiracy theories and misinformation spread unchecked, fueling further polarization.

Efforts to promote constructive dialogue and bridge partisan divides gained urgency in the wake of January 6. Civil society organizations, religious leaders, and community activists worked to create spaces for dialogue and reconciliation, encouraging Americans to listen to each other with empathy and understanding.

The legacy of January 6 underscored the importance of civility, decency, and inclusivity in public discourse and political engagement. It served as a reminder that democracy thrives on exchanging diverse perspectives and the ability to disagree respectfully. By fostering empathy, understanding, and mutual respect, Americans can work toward healing the divisions that threaten to tear the nation apart and rebuild trust in democratic institutions.

Impact on Democratic Resilience and Adaptation

The events of January 6, 2021, tested the resilience and adaptability of American democracy in the face of unprecedented challenges. This chapter explores how the attack on the U.S. Capitol forced democratic institutions and processes to adapt to new realities and threats, including increased security measures, changes to legislative procedures, and heightened vigilance against extremism. Efforts to strengthen democratic resilience gained momentum, focusing on promoting innovation, flexibility, and responsiveness in governance. The legacy of January 6 underscored the ability of American democracy to withstand external shocks and adapt to evolving threats while remaining true to its foundational principles.

The attack on the U.S. Capitol on January 6, 2021, was a wake-up call for American democracy, prompting a reevaluation of its resilience and capacity to withstand internal threats. The unprecedented breach of the Capitol forced democratic institutions and processes to adapt quickly to new realities and security challenges.

In response to the attack, security measures at the Capitol and other government buildings were significantly heightened. Law enforcement agencies implemented stricter protocols, deployed additional personnel, and fortified barriers to prevent future breaches. These measures aimed to safeguard democratic institutions and protect elected officials, staff, and visitors from harm.

The events of January 6 also prompted changes to legislative procedures and protocols to ensure the continuity of government operations in the face of potential disruptions. Lawmakers revisited emergency response plans, contingency measures, and succession protocols to address vulnerabilities exposed by the attack.

Efforts to strengthen democratic resilience extended beyond physical security to include measures aimed at countering extremism and safeguarding democratic norms and values. Governments, civil society organizations, and community leaders worked to promote civic education, media literacy, and critical thinking skills to inoculate citizens against disinformation and manipulation.

The legacy of January 6 underscored the adaptability and resilience of American democracy in the face of adversity. Despite the challenges posed by the attack, democratic institutions could respond effectively to threats and adapt to new realities. By promoting innovation, flexibility, and responsiveness in governance, American democracy demonstrated its ability to withstand external shocks and remain true to its foundational principles of freedom, equality, and justice.

Impact on Global Perception of American Democracy

January 6, 2021's legacy also affected the global perception of American democracy and leadership. This chapter explores how the attack on the U.S. Capitol raised questions about the stability and credibility of American democracy, as well as its ability to serve as a model for other nations. Efforts to rebuild America's standing on the world stage gained urgency, with a focus on promoting democratic values, human rights, and the rule of law in international relations. The legacy of January 6 underscored the importance of restoring America's reputation as a beacon of democracy and defending democratic institutions and norms worldwide.

The attack on the U.S. Capitol on January 6, 2021, sent shockwaves around the world and prompted a reassessment of global perceptions of American democracy. The scenes of violence and chaos played out on the world stage raised serious questions about the stability and credibility of democratic governance in the United States.

Many international observers expressed concern about the state of American democracy, with some questioning the country's ability to serve as a model for others. The attack on the U.S. Capitol was seen as a profound blow to America's image as a beacon of democracy and a defender of human rights and the rule of law.

In response to the events of January 6, efforts to rebuild America's standing on the world stage gained urgency. The Biden administration, in particular, prioritized restoring America's reputation as a champion of democratic values and human rights in international relations.

Diplomatic efforts were intensified to reaffirm America's commitment to democracy and strengthen partnerships with like-minded countries and organizations worldwide. The United States sought to lead by example, demonstrating its resilience and resolve in adversity.

The legacy of January 6 underscored the importance of defending democratic institutions and norms at home and abroad. America's credibility as a global leader and advocate for democracy hinged on its ability to address internal challenges and uphold its founding principles on the world stage. By reaffirming its commitment to democratic values, human rights, and the rule of law, the United States sought to regain the trust and confidence of the international community and to lead in advancing the cause of freedom and democracy worldwide.

Serving as a Cautionary Tale

Overall, the legacy of January 6, 2021, will continue to shape American politics, society, and democracy for years to come. This chapter delves into how the events of that day serve as a cautionary tale about the dangers of political extremism, the consequences of polarization, and the importance of defending democratic values and institutions. As the nation grapples with the aftermath of the insurrection, it must confront these challenges head-on and work together to build a more resilient and inclusive democracy for future generations.

The January 6, 2021, events left an indelible mark on American society, sparking a national reckoning with the state of democracy and the forces threatening its stability. The attack on the U.S. Capitol served as a stark reminder of the dangers posed by political extremism and the fragility of democratic institutions in the face of internal threats.

The legacy of January 6 is a cautionary tale about the dangers of political polarization and the corrosive effects of divisive rhetoric and misinformation. It laid bare the consequences of unchecked partisanship and the erosion of trust in democratic norms and institutions.

In the aftermath of the insurrection, there is a renewed sense of urgency about the need to defend democratic values and institutions from internal and external threats. Efforts to strengthen electoral integrity, safeguard civil liberties, and promote civic engagement have gained momentum as the nation seeks to fortify its democratic foundations.

At the same time, the legacy of January 6 has prompted soul-searching about the meaning of citizenship and patriotism in a diverse and divided society. It has challenged Americans to confront uncomfortable truths about the state of the nation and their role in shaping its future.

As the nation confronts these challenges, there is a growing recognition of the need for collective action and collaboration to build a more resilient and inclusive democracy. The events of January 6 have galvanized citizens from all walks of life to come together to defend democratic values and principles.

In the years to come, the legacy of January 6 will continue to shape American politics, society, and democracy. It will serve as a reminder of the importance of vigilance, resilience, and unity in the face of threats to democracy. By confronting these challenges head-on and working together to build a more robust and inclusive democracy, Americans can ensure that the events of January 6 serve as a turning point toward a brighter future for the nation.

TRUMP'S FAKE MEDIA CAMPAIGN

Donald Trump's reliance on what he dubbed "fake news" was like a puzzle piece he often used to shape the narrative of his presidential campaigns and time in office. This strategy drew much attention and criticism, becoming a central element of his political communication style.

Trump's use of fake news was like playing a puzzle game where he strategically placed misleading information to influence public opinion and discredit reports that didn't align with his agenda. He utilized this tactic to maintain support from his political base and deflect criticism.

One notable example of Trump's use of fake news was his repeated claims that mainstream media outlets were spreading false information about him and his administration. He often accused these outlets of being biased and motivated by political agendas, labeling them as "fake news" to undermine their credibility.

Additionally, Trump himself was not immune to spreading misinformation. He often shared unverified or misleading information on his social media platforms, amplifying conspiracy theories and baseless claims to his millions of followers.

Another example was during his presidential campaigns when he would make unsubstantiated claims about his opponents, casting doubt on their integrity and character. By framing them as untrustworthy or corrupt, he aimed to sway public opinion in his favor.

Despite facing criticism for his use of fake news, Trump continued to employ this tactic throughout his presidency. It became a defining feature of his communication strategy, contributing to the polarized media landscape and ongoing debates about the role of truth in politics.

False Allegations Against Opponents

Trump's strategy of spreading false allegations against his political opponents was akin to fitting puzzle pieces together to paint a negative image of them in the eyes of the public. Throughout his 2016 presidential campaign and subsequent years in office, he frequently employed this tactic to discredit his rivals and bolster his standing.

One of the most notable instances of Trump's use of false allegations was his relentless attacks on Hillary Clinton, his opponent in the 2016 presidential race. Trump famously dubbed her "Crooked Hillary" and accused her of a litany of offenses, ranging from mishandling classified information to engaging in corrupt dealings with foreign governments.

Despite lacking credible evidence to support these claims, Trump repeatedly echoed them at campaign rallies, on social media, and during televised interviews. By doing so, he aimed to tarnish Clinton's reputation and undermine her credibility in the eyes of voters.

For instance, Trump's accusations regarding Clinton's handling of classified information stemmed from her use of a private email server during her time as Secretary of State. While this issue was subject to investigation, no charges were ultimately brought against Clinton, and multiple inquiries concluded that she had not committed any criminal wrongdoing. However, Trump continued exploiting the controversy by doubting her trustworthiness.

Similarly, Trump propagated unfounded allegations of corruption against Clinton, suggesting that she had engaged in illicit dealings with foreign governments in exchange for personal gain. Any credible evidence did not substantiate these claims. Yet, they persisted throughout the campaign, feeding into negative perceptions of Clinton among specific segments of the electorate.

Overall, Trump's use of false allegations against his opponents was a deliberate strategy to manipulate public opinion and gain a competitive advantage in the political arena. While it sparked controversy and criticism, particularly from Clinton and her supporters, it nonetheless significantly shaped the discourse surrounding the 2016 presidential election.

Misleading Statements and Exaggerations

Trump's penchant for misleading statements and exaggerations was a puzzle piece in his broader strategy to enhance his image and tout his administration's accomplishments. He often selectively highlighted positive economic indicators throughout his office while downplaying or ignoring less flattering aspects of his administration's performance.

One area where Trump frequently exaggerated his achievements was the economy. He consistently touted job creation numbers and GDP growth rates as evidence of his success in revitalizing the economy. While these metrics did show improvement during his presidency, Trump often failed to acknowledge other factors, such as income inequality or the national debt, that painted a less rosy picture.

For example, Trump would boast about record-low unemployment rates, conveniently omitting the fact that wage growth remained stagnant for many American workers and that income inequality continued to widen. Similarly, he would celebrate substantial GDP growth numbers without acknowledging the ballooning national debt or the negative impact of his trade policies on specific sectors of the economy.

Trump's tendency to exaggerate his achievements and downplay his failures was not limited to economic issues. He also made misleading statements on immigration to healthcare, often painting an overly optimistic picture of his administration's actions and policies.

For instance, Trump frequently exaggerated the effectiveness of his immigration policies, claiming credit for reductions in illegal border crossings while ignoring the humanitarian crises that unfolded at the border under his watch. Similarly, he would boast about his efforts to repeal and replace the Affordable Care Act despite failing to deliver on his campaign promise to provide a better alternative.

Overall, Trump's use of misleading statements and exaggerations was a central feature of his political rhetoric, contributing to the proliferation of false or misleading information during his time in office. While his supporters praised his willingness to challenge the status quo and speak bluntly, critics argued that his disregard for facts and evidence undermined public trust in the presidency and democratic institutions.

Promotion of Conspiracy Theories

Trump's promotion of conspiracy theories during his presidency was like adding puzzling pieces to an already complex political landscape, stirring controversy and fueling distrust in the electoral process. Through his Twitter account and public appearances, he frequently amplified unfounded claims and baseless allegations, contributing to a climate of suspicion and division.

One particularly notable example of Trump's propagation of conspiracy theories occurred in the aftermath of the 2020 presidential election. Despite no credible evidence of widespread voter fraud, Trump repeatedly insisted that the election had been "rigged" against him and that millions of illegal votes had been cast. He used his platform to spread these claims, casting doubt on the legitimacy of the election results and sowing discord among his supporters.

Trump's insistence on the existence of voter fraud - despite numerous court rulings and investigations finding no evidence to support his claims - had far-reaching consequences. It undermined public trust in the electoral process. It fueled baseless allegations of wrongdoing, leading to heightened tensions and protests in some parts of the country.

Moreover, Trump's promotion of conspiracy theories extended beyond elections. He was known to endorse various other unfounded claims, including those related to the origins of the COVID-19 pandemic, the existence of a "deep state" within the government, and the alleged involvement of political rivals in criminal activities.

By lending credence to these conspiracy theories, Trump exacerbated existing divisions within society and eroded confidence in the institutions meant to uphold democratic norms and principles. His willingness to peddle falsehoods for political gain underscored the challenges posed by the spread of misinformation in the digital age. It highlighted the importance of critical thinking and media literacy in discerning fact from fiction.

Attacks on the Media

Trump's attacks on the mainstream media were akin to inserting puzzle pieces that painted the media as adversaries in a larger narrative, seeking to discredit critical coverage of his administration and shape public perception in his favor. Throughout his presidency, he repeatedly labeled reputable news outlets as "fake news" and "the enemy of the people," attempting to undermine their credibility and dismiss unfavorable reporting as biased or inaccurate.

By casting doubt on the integrity of the media, Trump aimed to control the narrative and shield himself from criticism. He often used his Twitter account and public appearances to denigrate journalists and news organizations that published stories critical of him or his administration. This tactic sought to discredit specific reports and delegitimize the entire media establishment in the eyes of his supporters.

One of the key motivations behind Trump's attacks on the media was to rally his base against what he portrayed as a biased and hostile press. By framing the media as adversaries, Trump sought to foster a sense of solidarity among his supporters and create an us-versus-them dynamic that reinforced his political agenda.

Moreover, Trump's attacks on the media served to erode public trust in journalism and undermine the essential role of a free and independent press in a democratic society. By sowing doubt about the integrity of news reporting, he contributed to a climate of skepticism and cynicism that made it increasingly difficult for the public to discern fact from fiction.

Despite widespread criticism for his attacks on the media, Trump remained steadfast in his efforts to control the narrative and shape public opinion. His tactics underscored the media's challenges in an era of heightened polarization. They demonstrated the importance of defending press freedom as a cornerstone of democracy.

Manipulation of Social Media

Trump's manipulation of social media, primarily through his prolific use of Twitter, was like placing puzzle pieces strategically to disseminate his messages and attack his critics. Throughout his presidency, Trump and his campaign team leveraged social media platforms to amplify their messaging and directly reach his millions of followers.

Trump's Twitter account, in particular, emerged as a powerful tool for him to communicate with his base and shape the public discourse. He frequently used the platform to disseminate false or misleading information, often without regard for accuracy or truthfulness. From baseless claims about voter fraud to personal attacks on political opponents and media figures, Trump's tweets were a constant source of controversy and division.

Despite Twitter's attempts to label or fact-check misleading tweets, Trump's online presence remained a potent source of misinformation. His tweets often went unchecked and unchallenged, allowing him to spread falsehoods with impunity to his vast audience.

One key strategy that Trump employed on social media was to bypass traditional media channels and communicate directly with his supporters. By doing so, he could control the narrative and circumvent critical coverage from mainstream news outlets. This direct communication also allowed Trump to rally his base, mobilize supporters, and shape public opinion unprecedentedly for a sitting president.

Moreover, Trump's manipulation of social media contributed to the erosion of trust in traditional institutions and the proliferation of misinformation online. By exploiting the reach and immediacy of platforms like Twitter, he was able to amplify his messages and sow doubt about the integrity of mainstream news reporting.

Overall, Trump's manipulation of social media was a central feature of his presidency, enabling him to disseminate false or misleading information and shape the political landscape in ways that will have lasting implications for the future of American democracy.

Misrepresentation of Scientific Facts

Trump's misrepresentation of scientific facts during the COVID-19 pandemic was like placing puzzle pieces that distorted the accurate picture of the situation, leading to confusion and undermining efforts to combat the virus effectively. Throughout the pandemic, Trump faced criticism for downplaying the severity of COVID-19 and spreading misinformation about the virus and potential treatments.

One of the most notable examples of Trump's misrepresentation of scientific facts was his promotion of unproven remedies, such as hydroxychloroquine, as a treatment for COVID-19. Despite lacking scientific evidence supporting its efficacy, Trump touted the drug as a potential "game-changer" and encouraged its use, both publicly and through his social media channels.

Trump's dismissal of expert advice and reliance on unproven treatments contributed to public confusion. It undermined efforts to combat the pandemic effectively. His statements often contradicted guidance from public health officials and scientific experts, creating a disjointed response to the crisis and eroding public trust in official information sources.

Furthermore, Trump's downplaying of the severity of COVID-19 and his reluctance to implement stringent public health measures, such as mask mandates and social distancing guidelines, sent mixed messages to the public and hindered efforts to control the spread of the virus.

Overall, Trump's misrepresentation of scientific facts during the COVID-19 pandemic exacerbated an already challenging situation, prolonging the pandemic's impact and undermining public health efforts. His dismissal of expert advice and promotion of unproven remedies highlighted the dangers of politicizing public health issues and the importance of relying on evidence-based approaches to combat infectious diseases.

False Claims About Immigration

Trump's false claims about immigration served as puzzle pieces in his efforts to justify his administration's policies and bolster support for initiatives such as the construction of a border wall between the United States and Mexico. Throughout his presidency, Trump frequently made exaggerated or misleading statements about immigration, painting immigrants as criminals and threats to national security.

One of the most prominent false claims made by Trump was his assertion that immigrants, particularly those entering the country illegally, were responsible for a disproportionate amount of crime. Despite numerous studies and data showing that immigrants commit crimes at lower rates than native-born citizens, Trump repeatedly conflated immigration with criminality, perpetuating stereotypes and stoking fear among the public.

Furthermore, Trump often used inflammatory rhetoric to characterize immigrants as invaders and threats to American sovereignty. He frequently invoked imagery of violence and lawlessness to justify his administration's hardline immigration policies, including the separation of families at the border and the implementation of strict immigration enforcement measures.

Trump's false claims about immigration not only misrepresented the facts but also fueled xenophobia and anti-immigrant sentiment among his supporters. By demonizing immigrants and portraying them as a threat to national security, Trump sought to rally his base and garner support for his agenda, including the construction of a border wall.

Despite facing criticism from advocacy groups and political opponents, Trump remained steadfast in his portrayal of immigration as a crisis requiring drastic measures. His administration's policies, informed by these false claims, had far-reaching consequences for immigrant communities and the broader discourse surrounding immigration in the United States.

Overall, Trump's false claims about immigration underscored the dangers of using misinformation to justify policy decisions and perpetuate harmful stereotypes. By exploiting public fears and misconceptions about immigration, Trump sought to advance his political agenda at the expense of vulnerable immigrant populations.

Revisionist History and Denial of Reality

Trump's penchant for revisionist history and denial of reality was like fitting puzzling pieces together to create a narrative that served his political agenda. Throughout his presidency, Trump was known for rewriting history and exaggerating his accomplishments, often to bolster his image and discredit his critics.

One prominent example of Trump's revisionist history was his tendency to claim credit for achievements before he took office. Whether it was economic growth, job creation, or international agreements, Trump often exaggerated his role in these successes, ignoring the contributions of previous administrations or external factors beyond his control.

Additionally, Trump was not shy about exaggerating the impact of his policies and initiatives. From tax cuts to deregulation efforts, he frequently touted these measures as unprecedented successes despite evidence to the contrary. Trump's propensity to distort facts and inflate his achievements contributed to a climate of skepticism and cynicism, eroding public trust in institutions and undermining the credibility of objective reality.

Moreover, Trump's denial of reality extended beyond his accomplishments to broader issues facing the country. Whether it was climate change, the COVID-19 pandemic, or racial injustice, Trump often downplayed or dismissed inconvenient truths that contradicted his worldview or political agenda.

For instance, Trump repeatedly questioned the scientific consensus on climate change, labeling it a "hoax" perpetuated by political opponents and the media. Similarly, he downplayed the severity of the COVID-19 pandemic, contradicting public health experts and spreading misinformation about the virus and potential treatments.

Overall, Trump's revisionist history and denial of reality had far-reaching consequences for public discourse and democratic norms. By distorting facts and rewriting history to suit his political agenda, he undermined the credibility of objective reality. He eroded public trust in institutions, further polarizing an already divided nation.

Conspiracy Theories and Dog Whistles

Trump's engagement with conspiracy theories and use of dog whistles served as puzzling pieces that appealed to fringe elements of his base, perpetuating divisive narratives and contributing to political polarization. Throughout his presidency, Trump frequently trafficked in conspiracy theories and employed coded language to signal support for extremist groups.

One of the most notable examples of Trump's promotion of conspiracy theories was his repeated claims of widespread voter fraud, particularly during the 2020 presidential election. Despite lacking evidence to support these claims, Trump continued to insist that the election had been "stolen" from him, fueling mistrust in the electoral process and undermining faith in democratic institutions.

Additionally, Trump often invoked the idea of a "deep state" – a shadowy network of government officials and bureaucrats allegedly working to undermine his presidency. While there may be legitimate concerns about government accountability and transparency, Trump's use of the term "deep state" served as a dog whistle to conspiracy theorists and far-right extremists, reinforcing their belief in a sinister plot against him.

Furthermore, Trump's willingness to embrace conspiracy theories extended to other issues, such as the COVID-19 pandemic and the origins of the virus. Despite the lack of evidence to support these assertions, he frequently promoted baseless claims about the virus being a "hoax" or deliberately engineered in a lab.

In addition to promoting conspiracy theories, Trump often used coded language to appeal to extremist groups within his base. Whether it was referring to immigrants as "invaders" or characterizing protests against racial injustice as "law and order" issues, Trump's rhetoric served to inflame tensions and deepen divisions within society.

Overall, Trump's engagement with conspiracy theories and use of dog whistles contributed to the normalization of extremist beliefs and attitudes. By legitimizing fringe ideas and signaling support for extremist groups, Trump encouraged far-right extremists and further polarized an already divided political landscape.

Selective Use of Information

Trump's selective use of information was like fitting puzzle pieces together to construct a narrative that suited his political agenda, often at the expense of objective truth. Throughout his presidency, Trump and his allies frequently cherry-picked or ignored evidence to support their arguments, particularly on contentious issues such as climate change.

One of the most glaring examples of Trump's selective use of information was his dismissal of scientific consensus on climate change. Despite overwhelming evidence from the scientific community pointing to the reality of global warming and its potentially catastrophic consequences, Trump consistently downplayed the threat of climate change and cast doubt on its human-caused origins.

Instead of acknowledging the urgency of addressing climate change, Trump and his allies selectively cited data and studies that aligned with their skepticism or denial of the issue. They often emphasized uncertainties in climate science or highlighted isolated incidents of extreme weather events to argue against taking decisive action to mitigate climate change.

Moreover, Trump's administration rolled back environmental regulations. It withdrew from international agreements to combat climate change, further underscoring his administration's disregard for scientific evidence and the urgent need for action.

Beyond climate change, Trump's selective use of information was evident in debates over other pressing issues, such as healthcare and immigration. He and his allies often exaggerated the benefits of their policies while downplaying or ignoring the potential negative consequences, shaping public perception to align with their political objectives.

Overall, Trump's selective use of information undermined public trust in institutions and eroded the credibility of objective truth. By ignoring or distorting inconvenient facts, he sought to advance his political agenda and downplay the urgency of addressing pressing issues, contributing to a climate of misinformation and polarization in American politics.

Attacks on the Media

Trump's attacks on the mainstream media were akin to placing puzzle pieces that aimed to delegitimize critical reporting and sow doubt in journalistic institutions. Throughout his presidency, Trump repeatedly targeted the media, labeling reputable news outlets as "fake news" and "the enemy of the people."

By dismissing unfavorable coverage as fake news, Trump sought to shield himself from criticism and create a narrative of media bias among his supporters. He portrayed the media as partisan and dishonest, accusing journalists of intentionally spreading misinformation to undermine his presidency.

One of the key motivations behind Trump's attacks on the media was to discredit critical reporting and control the narrative surrounding his administration. By undermining the media's credibility, Trump sought to shape public perception and shield himself from accountability for his actions and policies.

Moreover, Trump's attacks on the media were often accompanied by attempts to silence dissenting voices and suppress freedom of the press. He frequently targeted individual journalists and news organizations with personal attacks and threats of legal action, further eroding press freedom and chilling investigative journalism.

Despite widespread criticism for his attacks on the media, Trump remained steadfast in his efforts to undermine journalistic institutions and shape public opinion. His rhetoric contributed to a climate of hostility and mistrust toward the media, exacerbating existing societal divisions.

Overall, Trump's attacks on the media were a central feature of his presidency, highlighting the importance of a free and independent press in holding those in power accountable. By dismissing critical reporting as fake news, Trump sought to manipulate public perception and shield himself from scrutiny, undermining the principles of democracy and the role of journalism in a free society.

Promotion of False Voter Fraud Claims

Trump's promotion of false voter fraud claims following his loss in the 2020 presidential election was like fitting puzzle pieces together to construct a narrative that challenged the legitimacy of the election results. Despite lacking evidence to support their allegations, Trump and his allies repeatedly insisted that the election had been "stolen" from him, perpetuating baseless conspiracy theories and undermining confidence in the electoral process.

From the moment it became clear that he had lost the election, Trump and his supporters began spreading unfounded claims of widespread voter fraud. They alleged that mail-in ballots were fraudulent, voting machines were rigged, and illegal votes had been cast on a massive scale, despite numerous investigations and court rulings finding no evidence to support these claims.

Trump's insistence on the existence of voter fraud was reflected in his decision to file numerous legal challenges in battleground states, seeking to overturn the election results. However, most of these lawsuits were dismissed by judges, often due to lack of evidence or procedural flaws.

Despite the lack of credible evidence, Trump continued to promote false voter fraud claims through his social media channels and public statements, fueling conspiracy theories and eroding public trust in the electoral process. His refusal to accept the election's outcome and his efforts to overturn the results had far-reaching consequences for American democracy, exacerbating societal divisions and undermining faith in the integrity of the electoral system.

Moreover, Trump's promotion of false voter fraud claims had real-world consequences, contributing to a climate of mistrust and uncertainty surrounding the election outcome. It also could undermine future elections by sowing doubt in voters' minds and casting doubt on the legitimacy of the democratic process.

Overall, Trump's promotion of false voter fraud claims following the 2020 presidential election was a troubling example of his willingness to prioritize his political interests over the principles of democracy and the rule of law. By perpetuating baseless conspiracy theories and eroding confidence in the electoral process, Trump posed a significant threat to the foundations of American democracy.

Misleading Statements About Economic Achievements

Trump's frequent boasting about economic achievements during his presidency was like fitting puzzle pieces together to construct a narrative of success, often at the expense of accuracy and context. While Trump consistently touted job growth and stock market gains as evidence of his economic prowess, economists and fact-checkers pointed out that many of his claims were misleading or exaggerated.

One of the key criticisms of Trump's economic claims was his tendency to take credit for economic trends that began under his predecessor, Barack Obama. When Trump took office in January 2017, he inherited a strong economy with low unemployment and steady GDP growth. However, rather than acknowledging the progress made during the Obama administration, Trump often exaggerated his role in economic growth and downplayed the challenges faced by working-class Americans.

For example, Trump frequently touted the low unemployment rate as evidence of his successful economic policies, ignoring that the unemployment rate had steadily declined since the Great Recession. Similarly, he took credit for stock market gains even though the stock market had been trending upward for years before his presidency.

Moreover, Trump's economic policies, such as tax cuts and deregulation, disproportionately benefited corporations and the wealthy rather than working-class Americans. While Trump claimed that his policies would spur economic growth and benefit all Americans, critics argued that they exacerbated income inequality and failed to address structural issues facing the economy, such as stagnant wages and rising healthcare costs.

Overall, Trump's misleading statements about economic achievements reflected his penchant for self-promotion and his willingness to distort facts to advance his political agenda. By exaggerating his role in economic growth and downplaying the challenges facing working-class Americans, Trump sought to bolster his image as a successful businessman and leader despite evidence to the contrary.

Promotion of False Health Claims

Trump's promotion of false health claims during the COVID-19 pandemic was like fitting puzzle pieces together to create a dangerous and misleading narrative about potential treatments. Despite warnings from health experts, Trump repeatedly suggested unproven and even dangerous methods for treating COVID-19, contributing to public confusion and undermining efforts to control the spread of the virus.

One of the most alarming examples of Trump's promotion of false health claims was his suggestion that injecting disinfectants or using ultraviolet light could cure COVID-19. During a press briefing in April 2020, Trump mused about the possibility of using disinfectants or ultraviolet light to kill the virus inside the body, prompting swift condemnation from health experts who warned that such methods were ineffective and potentially harmful.

Trump's remarks sparked widespread backlash and led to a surge in calls to poison control centers from people seeking guidance on ingesting disinfectants. The manufacturers of disinfectants were also forced to issue statements warning against improper use of their products, further highlighting the dangers of Trump's irresponsible comments.

Moreover, Trump promoted unproven health remedies beyond disinfectants and ultraviolet light. He also touted the anti-malarial drug hydroxychloroquine as a potential treatment for COVID-19 despite limited evidence of its effectiveness and concerns about its safety.

Trump's promotion of unproven health remedies not only misled the public but also undermined efforts to control the spread of the virus. By spreading misinformation about potential treatments, Trump contributed to confusion and eroded trust in public health authorities and scientific expertise.

Overall, Trump's promotion of false health claims during the COVID-19 pandemic underscored the dangers of politicizing public health issues and the importance of relying on evidence-based approaches to combatting infectious diseases. His disregard for scientific evidence and willingness to promote unproven treatments had real-world consequences, highlighting the need for responsible leadership in times of crisis.

Misrepresentation of Foreign Policy Achievements

Trump's misrepresentation of his administration's foreign policy achievements was like placing puzzle pieces together to create a narrative of success that often diverged from reality. Throughout his presidency, Trump frequently exaggerated his accomplishments on the global stage while downplaying or ignoring his administration's failures.

One of the most prominent examples of Trump's misrepresentation of foreign policy achievements was his claim to have achieved "historic" peace agreements in the Middle East. Trump touted agreements between Israel and several Arab states, such as the Abraham Accords, as groundbreaking diplomatic achievements that would bring lasting peace to the region. However, critics argued that these agreements were largely symbolic and did not address the underlying conflicts and tensions in the Middle East.

While the Abraham Accords represented a significant step toward normalization of relations between Israel and its Arab neighbors, they did not address critical issues such as the Israeli-Palestinian conflict or the ongoing humanitarian crisis in Gaza. Moreover, some analysts questioned the long-term sustainability of the agreements and their impact on regional stability.

Despite these criticisms, Trump continued exaggerating his administration's foreign policy successes, portraying himself as a master dealmaker and diplomat. Despite evidence to the contrary, he frequently claimed to have achieved more than any of his predecessors on the world stage.

Moreover, Trump's misrepresentation of foreign policy achievements distorted public perception of his administration's record on international affairs. By exaggerating his successes and downplaying his failures, Trump sought to bolster his image as a strong and effective leader despite the complexities and challenges of global diplomacy.

Overall, Trump's tendency to misrepresent his administration's foreign policy achievements underscored the dangers of relying on political spin and exaggeration to shape public opinion. By distorting the reality of his administration's record on international affairs, Trump undermined public trust in the credibility of government and contributed to a climate of misinformation and uncertainty.

Denial of Negative Reports

Trump's dismissal of adverse reports as "fake news" was like fitting puzzle pieces together to create a narrative that discredited critical journalism and shielded him from scrutiny. Throughout his presidency, Trump consistently used the term "fake news" to delegitimize journalists and media outlets that portrayed him unfavorably, often in an attempt to deflect attention from damaging revelations or allegations.

One of the most notable examples of Trump's denial of adverse reports was his response to allegations of collusion with Russia during the 2016 election. Despite mounting evidence suggesting possible ties between his campaign and Russian officials, Trump repeatedly denounced these allegations as "fake news" and a "witch hunt." He accused the media of spreading false information and bias against him despite the ongoing investigations by independent counsel Robert Mueller and the intelligence community.

By labeling reports of collusion as fake news, Trump sought to undermine their credibility and portray himself as the victim of a partisan smear campaign. His attacks on the media served to rally his base and discredit critical reporting despite the seriousness of the allegations and the potential implications for national security.

Moreover, Trump's dismissal of adverse reports as fake news extended beyond the issue of collusion with Russia. He routinely used the term to denounce critical coverage of his administration's policies, personal conduct, and controversies, casting doubt on the credibility of journalists and media outlets that challenged his narrative.

Overall, Trump's denial of adverse reports as fake news was a central feature of his presidency, highlighting his disdain for accountability and transparency. By labeling critical journalism as fake, Trump sought to undermine public trust in the media and shape the narrative to suit his political interests, regardless of the facts or evidence.

Promotion of Conspiracy Theories

Trump's promotion of conspiracy theories was like adding puzzling pieces to a narrative that blurred the lines between fact and fiction, often leading to widespread misinformation and uncertainty among his followers. Throughout his time in office, Trump frequently amplified conspiracy theories through his social media platforms, using his massive online presence to propagate false and baseless claims.

One of the most notorious examples of Trump's promotion of conspiracy theories was his role in popularizing the "birther" conspiracy theory, which falsely claimed that President Barack Obama was not born in the United States and, therefore, ineligible to serve as president. Trump played a significant role in spreading this baseless theory, repeatedly questioning Obama's citizenship and demanding to see his birth certificate.

Despite lacking any credible evidence to support his claims, Trump's promotion of the birther conspiracy theory gained traction among some segments of the population. It fueled doubts about Obama's legitimacy as president. However, after years of promoting the theory, Trump later distanced himself from it without formally apologizing or acknowledging the harm it caused.

In addition to the birther conspiracy theory, Trump has amplified a wide range of other conspiracy theories throughout his presidency, including claims about voter fraud, the COVID-19 pandemic, and the existence of a "deep state" within the government. By crediting these baseless claims, Trump further sowed doubt and confusion among his followers, undermining public trust in institutions and contributing to political polarization.

Overall, Trump's promotion of conspiracy theories has had far-reaching consequences for public discourse and democratic norms. By spreading misinformation and questioning the legitimacy of political opponents, Trump undermined the integrity of the electoral process and eroded public trust in the foundations of democracy.

Selective Use of Information

Trump's selective use of information was like piecing together a puzzle to construct a narrative that favored his agenda while disregarding inconvenient truths. Throughout his presidency, Trump frequently cherry-picked facts and data to support his claims of success, contributing to a distorted narrative that fueled polarization and undermined public trust in institutions.

One prominent example of Trump's selective use of information was his manipulation of crime statistics to bolster his claims of success in combating crime. Despite the overall decline in crime rates during his presidency, Trump often exaggerated the extent of these declines and cherry-picked specific statistics to paint a rosy picture of law and order under his administration. He frequently touted decreases in certain types of crime, such as homicides or illegal border crossings, while ignoring or downplaying increases in other areas, such as hate crimes or domestic terrorism.

Similarly, Trump selectively highlighted economic indicators that supported his narrative of a booming economy while ignoring or downplaying economic inequality or hardship indicators. He frequently touted low unemployment rates and stock market gains as evidence of his administration's success while downplaying stagnant wages, rising income inequality, and other economic challenges faced by working-class Americans.

Moreover, Trump's selective use of information extended beyond crime and the economy to other areas of policy and governance. He frequently cherry-picked data to support his claims on issues such as immigration, healthcare, and foreign policy, creating a narrative that aligned with his political agenda while disregarding contradictory evidence.

Overall, Trump's selective use of information contributed to misinformation and polarization, undermining public trust in institutions and eroding the credibility of objective reality. By cherry-picking facts and data to support his claims of success, Trump perpetuated a distorted narrative that fueled societal divisions and hindered efforts to address the nation's pressing issues.

Attacks on Journalists and Media Outlets

Trump's relentless attacks on journalists and media outlets were like fitting puzzle pieces together to create a narrative that undermined press freedom and fostered a climate of distrust toward mainstream media. Throughout his presidency, Trump targeted journalists and media organizations that published critical stories about him, branding them as "enemy of the people" or "dishonest" in an attempt to discredit their reporting and shield himself from scrutiny.

One of the hallmarks of Trump's attacks on the media was his tendency to single out individual reporters or outlets for criticism, often in highly personal and derogatory terms. He frequently used his platform to denigrate journalists who challenged or questioned his actions, casting them as partisan actors or purveyors of fake news.

Moreover, Trump's attacks on journalists and media outlets were central to his broader strategy to undermine trust in mainstream media and promote alternative narratives aligned with his political agenda. By casting doubt on the credibility of critical reporting, Trump sought to create a climate of uncertainty and confusion among the public, making it easier for him to control the narrative and shape public opinion.

Trump's attacks on the media also had real-world consequences for journalists and reporters, who faced increased threats and harassment as a result of his rhetoric. According to the Committee to Protect Journalists, the United States saw a significant increase in attacks on journalists and media organizations during Trump's presidency, including physical assaults, threats of violence, and arrests.

Overall, Trump's attacks on journalists and media outlets were a dangerous assault on press freedom and the principles of democracy. By undermining the credibility of critical reporting and fostering a distrust toward mainstream media, Trump sought to silence dissent and consolidate his power, posing a significant threat to the integrity of democratic institutions and the free press.

Alternative Narratives and Alternative Facts

Trump's penchant for alternative narratives and facts was like fitting puzzle pieces together to construct a distorted reality that served his political agenda. Throughout his presidency, Trump and his administration frequently presented alternative narratives or facts to counter widely accepted truths or events, creating confusion and blurring the lines between reality and fiction.

One infamous example of Trump's use of alternative facts was his administration's exaggerated claims about the crowd size at his inauguration. Despite photographic evidence and aerial images clearly showing a smaller crowd than in previous inaugurations, Trump and his press secretary, Sean Spicer, insisted that the crowd was the largest in history. This blatant disregard for reality and insistence on promoting a false narrative undermined the administration's credibility from the outset.

Moreover, Trump's administration presented alternative narratives on various issues throughout his presidency, often in response to negative coverage or criticism. Whether it was downplaying the severity of the COVID-19 pandemic, disputing the results of the 2020 presidential election, or spreading misinformation about immigration, Trump and his allies- frequently sought to create doubt and confusion by presenting alternative facts that contradicted established truths.

The use of alternative narratives and facts by Trump and his administration had far-reaching consequences for public discourse and democratic norms. By blurring the lines between reality and fiction, they undermined the credibility of objective truth. They eroded public trust in institutions, including the media and government.

Overall, Trump's reliance on alternative narratives and facts reflected a dangerous disregard for the truth and a willingness to manipulate reality to suit his political agenda. By presenting a distorted version of events, Trump sought to sow confusion and undermine public confidence in the institutions and norms that underpin democracy, posing a significant threat to the integrity of American governance.

Denial of Negative Reports

Trump's dismissal of adverse reports as "fake news" was akin to fitting puzzle pieces together to create a narrative of doubt and confusion that shielded him from scrutiny and undermined the public's trust in the media. Throughout his presidency, Trump repeatedly labeled critical coverage as fake, aiming to discredit reputable news organizations and journalists and erode the public's confidence in the media's ability to hold elected officials accountable.

By dismissing adverse reports as fake news, Trump sought to create doubt and confusion among the public, casting doubt on the credibility of critical reporting and shielding himself from accountability. This tactic served to deflect attention away from the substance of the reports and focus instead on the perceived bias or agenda of the media outlets.

Moreover, Trump's repeated use of the term "fake news" had a corrosive effect on public discourse and democratic norms. By undermining the media's credibility, Trump eroded the public's trust in objective truth and fostered a climate of skepticism and cynicism.

Furthermore, Trump's dismissal of adverse reports as fake news had real-world consequences for journalists and media organizations. It fueled hostility toward reporters and led to an increase in threats and harassment directed at those who dared to challenge the administration's narrative.

Overall, Trump's denial of adverse reports as fake news was a dangerous assault on press freedom and the principles of democracy. By casting doubt on the credibility of critical reporting and undermining the public's trust in the media, Trump sought to evade accountability and consolidate his power, posing a significant threat to the integrity of democratic institutions and the free press.

Promotion of Conspiracy Theories

Trump's promotion of conspiracy theories through his social media platforms was like fitting puzzle pieces together to create a narrative of mistrust and division that undermined public discourse and eroded trust in institutions. Throughout his presidency, Trump's willingness to amplify baseless claims fueled division and sowed doubt in the minds of the American public.

One of the most notable examples of Trump's promotion of conspiracy theories was his role in popularizing the "birther" conspiracy theory, which falsely claimed that President Barack Obama was not born in the United States and, therefore, ineligible to serve as president. Despite lacking any credible evidence to support this claim, Trump relentlessly promoted the conspiracy theory, using his platform to question Obama's legitimacy as president and demand to see his birth certificate.

Trump's promotion of the birther conspiracy theory had harmful implications for public discourse and democratic norms. By giving credence to a baseless claim, Trump undermined the legitimacy of the Obama presidency and fueled racist narratives about Obama's citizenship and identity.

Moreover, Trump's willingness to exploit falsehoods for political gain extended beyond the birther conspiracy theory. Throughout his presidency, he frequently amplified conspiracy theories about issues such as voter fraud, the COVID-19 pandemic, and the existence of a "deep state" within the government, further eroding trust in institutions and fostering a climate of mistrust and division.

Overall, Trump's promotion of conspiracy theories profoundly impacted public discourse and democratic norms. By crediting baseless claims and fueling division and mistrust in institutions, Trump undermined the foundations of democracy and posed a significant threat to the integrity of American governance.

Selective Use of Information

Trump's selective use of information was akin to arranging puzzle pieces to construct a narrative reinforcing his political agenda, often at the expense of objective truth. Throughout his presidency, Trump consistently highlighted statistics or data that supported his claims while disregarding contradictory evidence, creating an echo chamber that reinforced his supporters' beliefs and contributed to the polarization of American society.

One of the key features of Trump's selective use of information was his tendency to emphasize positive indicators while downplaying or ignoring negative trends. For example, he frequently touted low unemployment rates and stock market gains as evidence of his administration's economic success while ignoring systemic issues such as income inequality or stagnant wages.

Moreover, Trump's selective use of information extended beyond economic indicators to other areas of policy and governance. He routinely cherry-picked data to support his claims on issues such as immigration, crime, and foreign policy, creating a distorted narrative that aligned with his political agenda while disregarding contradictory evidence.

By selectively using information to reinforce his political agenda, Trump created an echo chamber that reinforced his supporters' beliefs and shielded them from alternative perspectives. This manipulation of facts hindered constructive dialogue on important issues and contributed to the growing polarization of American society.

Furthermore, Trump's selective use of information had real-world consequences for policy-making and public discourse. By ignoring or downplaying inconvenient facts, Trump hindered efforts to address pressing issues such as climate change, healthcare, and racial inequality, exacerbating existing divisions within society.

Overall, Trump's selective use of information was a dangerous assault on the principles of democracy and the integrity of public discourse. By manipulating facts to suit his political agenda, Trump undermined the credibility of objective truth and hindered efforts to address the nation's pressing challenges.

Attacks on Journalists and Media Outlets

Trump's attacks on journalists and media outlets were like fitting puzzle pieces together to construct a narrative that undermined the credibility of the free press and intimidated dissenting voices. Throughout his presidency, Trump employed a calculated strategy to undermine the credibility of journalists and media organizations that criticized his administration, portraying them as the "enemy of the people" in an attempt to delegitimize their reporting and shield himself from accountability.

One of the key features of Trump's attacks on journalists and media outlets was his use of hostile rhetoric and personal attacks to discredit critical reporting. He routinely singled out individual reporters and media organizations for criticism, labeling them as "fake news" or "dishonest" whenever they published stories that portrayed him unfavorably.

Moreover, Trump's attacks on journalists and media outlets were often accompanied by attempts to intimidate and silence dissenting voices. He frequently threatened to revoke press credentials, sue media organizations, or retaliate against journalists who challenged him or questioned his actions, creating a climate of fear and intimidation within the media industry.

By portraying the media as the "enemy of the people," Trump sought to undermine the credibility of critical reporting and create a narrative of distrust and hostility toward journalists and media organizations. This hostile rhetoric endangered journalists and eroded public trust in the free press, a cornerstone of democratic governance.

Furthermore, Trump's attacks on journalists and media outlets had far-reaching consequences for press freedom and democratic norms. By undermining the credibility of the free press and intimidating dissenting voices, Trump posed a significant threat to the principles of transparency, accountability, and informed public discourse.

Overall, Trump's attacks on journalists and media outlets were a dangerous assault on press freedom and the principles of democracy. By portraying the media as the "enemy of the people" and seeking to delegitimize critical reporting, Trump undermined the foundations of democratic governance and posed a threat to the integrity of the free press.

Alternative Narratives and Alternative Facts

Trump's penchant for peddling alternative narratives and facts was akin to fitting puzzle pieces together to construct a distorted version of reality that served his political agenda. Throughout his presidency, Trump repeatedly presented conflicting accounts of events or distorted reality to exploit the public's susceptibility to misinformation, fueling confusion and undermining the credibility of objective truth.

One of the key features of Trump's use of alternative narratives and facts was his willingness to present conflicting accounts of events or distort reality to suit his political agenda. Whether it was downplaying the severity of the COVID-19 pandemic, disputing the results of the 2020 presidential election, or spreading misinformation about immigration, Trump consistently sought to create doubt and confusion by presenting alternative facts that contradicted established truths.

Moreover, Trump's use of alternative narratives and alternative facts empowered his supporters to dismiss inconvenient truths as partisan propaganda. By presenting conflicting accounts of events, Trump created a narrative of uncertainty and distrust that made it easier for his supporters to reject information that challenged their beliefs or contradicted his political agenda.

Furthermore, Trump's use of alternative narratives and alternative facts had far-reaching consequences for public discourse and democratic norms. By blurring the lines between truth and fiction, Trump undermined the credibility of objective truth and fostered a climate of misinformation and confusion that hindered efforts to address the nation's pressing issues.

Overall, Trump's willingness to peddle alternative narratives and facts significantly threatened the integrity of public discourse and democratic governance. By exploiting the public's susceptibility to misinformation and presenting conflicting accounts of events, Trump undermined the foundations of democracy and fueled confusion and distrust among the American public.

Manipulation of Social Media

Trump's mastery of social media platforms, especially Twitter, was like fitting puzzle pieces together to create a powerful tool for shaping the news cycle and controlling the narrative surrounding his presidency. Throughout his time in office, Trump's prolific use of Twitter allowed him to bypass traditional media channels and disseminate false or misleading information directly to his followers, amplifying his message and cultivating a loyal online following.

One of the key features of Trump's manipulation of social media was his ability to shape the news cycle and control the narrative surrounding his presidency. By using Twitter to make announcements, share policy decisions, and respond to criticism in real time, Trump was able to set the agenda for media coverage and dominate public discourse.

Moreover, Trump's use of Twitter to spread misinformation enabled him to amplify his message and reach a broad audience without the filter of traditional media gatekeepers. He frequently used his Twitter account to disseminate false or misleading information about issues such as voter fraud, the COVID-19 pandemic, and his political opponents, exploiting the platform's reach and immediacy to sow confusion and advance his political agenda.

Furthermore, Trump's social media manipulation had far-reaching consequences for public discourse and democratic norms. Using Twitter to spread misinformation and shape public opinion, Trump undermined the credibility of objective truth and fostered a climate of distrust and polarization that hindered efforts to address pressing issues facing the nation.

Overall, Trump's mastery of social media platforms, particularly Twitter, was a powerful tool for shaping public opinion and controlling the narrative surrounding his presidency. By leveraging social media to spread misinformation, Trump amplified his message and cultivated a loyal online following, posing a significant challenge to the integrity of public discourse and democratic governance.

Exploitation of Confirmation Bias

Trump's utilization of fake news tactics often preyed on confirmation bias, leveraging individuals' inclination to seek out information that reinforces their existing beliefs while disregarding contradictory evidence. By feeding his supporters a constant stream of misinformation that aligned with their preconceived notions, Trump deepened the partisan divide and reinforced ideological echo chambers, further entrenching polarization and hindering constructive dialogue.

One of the critical aspects of Trump's exploitation of confirmation bias was his strategic dissemination of misinformation that resonated with his supporters' beliefs and values. Through speeches, rallies, and social media posts, Trump consistently reinforced his followers' preconceptions by promoting narratives aligned with their worldview, regardless of their accuracy or veracity.

Moreover, Trump's manipulation of confirmation bias was evident in his attacks on the media as "fake news," which served to delegitimize critical reporting and reinforce his supporters' distrust of mainstream media outlets. By dismissing unfavorable coverage as biased or dishonest, Trump encouraged his supporters to seek out alternative sources of information that validated their beliefs, deepening the divide between competing ideological factions.

Furthermore, Trump's exploitation of confirmation bias exacerbated the problem of ideological echo chambers, wherein individuals are exposed only to information that confirms their existing beliefs, leading to a narrowing of perspectives and a lack of exposure to alternative viewpoints. By perpetuating a cycle of selective exposure to biased information, Trump hindered efforts to bridge the ideological divide and foster meaningful dialogue across political lines.

Overall, Trump's exploitation of confirmation bias was a central feature of his fake news tactics, enabling him to deepen the partisan divide and reinforce ideological echo chambers among his supporters. By strategically disseminating misinformation that aligned with their preconceived notions, Trump hindered efforts to foster constructive dialogue and compromise, exacerbating polarization and undermining the integrity of public discourse.

Undermining Trust in Institutions

Trump's relentless attacks on institutions such as the judiciary, intelligence agencies, and scientific experts constituted a systematic effort to undermine public trust in the fundamental pillars of democracy. By sowing doubt in the credibility of these institutions, he weakened their ability to serve as checks on executive power, ultimately eroding democratic norms and paving the way for authoritarian tendencies.

One of the key features of Trump's strategy was his consistent disparagement of institutions that he perceived as threats to his authority or agenda. Whether through tweets, speeches, or media appearances, Trump routinely attacked judges who ruled against his policies, intelligence agencies that contradicted his narratives, and scientists whose findings challenged his beliefs.

Moreover, Trump's attacks on these institutions often took the form of baseless accusations of bias, corruption, or incompetence, further undermining public trust in their integrity and credibility. By casting doubt on the motives and competence of judges, intelligence officials, and scientists, Trump sought to delegitimize their authority and erode public confidence in their ability to serve as impartial arbiters of truth and justice.

Furthermore, Trump's undermining of trust in institutions had far-reaching consequences for the rule of law and democratic governance. By weakening the credibility of the judiciary, intelligence agencies, and scientific experts, Trump hindered their ability to act as adequate checks on executive power, eroding the power balance and undermining democratic accountability.

Overall, Trump's relentless attacks on institutions were a dangerous assault on the foundations of democracy. By sowing doubt in the credibility of key democratic institutions, he weakened democratic norms. He paved the way for authoritarian tendencies, posing a significant threat to the rule of law and the integrity of democratic governance.

Normalization of Falsehoods

Trump's repeated dissemination of false or misleading information profoundly impacted public discourse, leading to the normalization of falsehoods and the erosion of trust in the integrity of information. Over time, this normalization contributed to a climate of cynicism and apathy, where the distinction between truth and fiction became increasingly blurred, and public discourse became less grounded in facts.

One of the critical aspects of Trump's normalization of falsehoods was his consistent pattern of spreading misinformation on a wide range of topics, from the economy to immigration to public health. Through speeches, interviews, and social media posts, Trump repeatedly made false or misleading claims, creating a narrative in which deception became an accepted part of political discourse.

Moreover, Trump's normalization of falsehoods was facilitated by his attacks on the media as "fake news," which served to undermine the credibility of critical reporting and reinforce his supporters' distrust of mainstream media outlets. By dismissing unfavorable coverage as biased or dishonest, Trump encouraged his supporters to seek out alternative sources of information that validated their beliefs, further contributing to the erosion of trust in the integrity of information.

Furthermore, Trump's normalization of falsehoods had far-reaching consequences for public discourse and democratic norms. By blurring the lines between truth and fiction, Trump undermined the foundations of democratic governance and paved the way for manipulation by those in positions of power. In a climate where falsehoods were normalized, facts became less important than the promoted narrative, making it easier for politicians and other actors to manipulate public opinion for their gain.

Overall, Trump's normalization of falsehoods was a dangerous assault on the integrity of public discourse and the foundations of democracy. By blurring the lines between truth and fiction and undermining trust in the integrity of information, Trump contributed to a climate of cynicism and apathy that weakened democratic norms and made the public more susceptible to manipulation by those in positions of power.

Legacy of Distrust

Trump's legacy of using fake news as a political weapon has left a profound and lasting impact on American democracy, contributing to the erosion of trust in media, institutions, and objective reality. This legacy poses a significant challenge to the health of democratic governance, as trust is essential for the functioning of democratic institutions and preserving democratic norms.

One of the critical aspects of Trump's legacy is the widespread erosion of trust in the media. By repeatedly attacking the media as "fake news" and spreading misinformation, Trump undermined the credibility of critical reporting and reinforced partisan divides, further polarizing public discourse and hindering efforts to find common ground on pressing issues.

Moreover, Trump's attacks on institutions such as the judiciary, intelligence agencies, and scientific experts contributed to a broader erosion of trust in the integrity of democratic institutions. By sowing doubt in the credibility of these institutions, Trump undermined their ability to serve as adequate checks on executive power, weakening democratic norms and eroding public confidence in the rule of law.

Furthermore, Trump's legacy of using fake news as a political weapon has contributed to a climate of confusion and uncertainty, where the distinction between truth and fiction has become increasingly blurred. This legacy has made it more difficult for citizens to discern fact from fiction. It has made them more susceptible to manipulation by those in positions of power.

Concerted efforts will be required To rebuild trust and restore integrity to public discourse from policymakers, journalists, and citizens. Policymakers must strengthen democratic institutions and uphold the rule of law. At the same time, journalists must redouble their efforts to hold those in power accountable and provide accurate and reliable information to the public. Additionally, citizens must actively engage in critical thinking and media literacy, questioning information sources and seeking diverse perspectives to better understand the world around them.

Overall, Trump's legacy of using fake news as a political weapon has left a profound impact on American democracy, posing a significant challenge to the health of democratic governance. Rebuilding trust and restoring integrity to public discourse will require sustained and concerted efforts from all segments of society.

Distracting from Policy Failures

Trump's utilization of accusations of fake news to divert attention from policy failures or controversies within his administration was a calculated strategy aimed at deflecting accountability and maintaining political support. When faced with criticism or negative coverage regarding issues such as healthcare reform, immigration policy, or economic downturns, Trump would often resort to accusing the media of spreading fake news, shifting the focus away from substantive issues and onto perceived biases within the media.

One of the critical aspects of Trump's strategy was his ability to use accusations of fake news to create a narrative in which the media was portrayed as the enemy of the people, working against the interests of the American public. By framing negative coverage as biased or dishonest, Trump sought to undermine the credibility of critical reporting and reinforce his narrative of victimization, deflecting attention from policy failures and controversies within his administration.

Moreover, Trump's use of accusations of fake news to distract from policy failures was facilitated by his mastery of social media and ability to communicate directly with his supporters. Through tweets and other social media posts, Trump could bypass traditional media channels and disseminate his message directly to his followers, reinforcing his narrative and maintaining political support despite negative coverage in the mainstream media.

Furthermore, Trump's use of accusations of fake news to distract from policy failures had far-reaching consequences for public discourse and democratic governance. By shifting the focus away from substantive issues and onto perceived biases within the media, Trump hindered efforts to hold his administration accountable for its actions and undermined the integrity of public discourse.

Overall, Trump's use of accusations of fake news to distract from policy failures was a calculated strategy aimed at deflecting accountability and maintaining political support. By framing negative coverage as biased or dishonest, Trump sought to undermine the credibility of critical reporting and reinforce his narrative of victimization, ultimately hindering efforts to address pressing issues facing the nation.

Gaslighting and Reality Distortion

Trump's utilization of fake news tactics extended beyond merely labeling unfavorable coverage as false; he engaged in gaslighting tactics to distort reality and manipulate public perception. Gaslighting involves denying or distorting reality to make one's version of events seem plausible, creating confusion and undermining people's ability to discern fact from fiction. Through gaslighting, Trump blurred the lines between reality and falsehood, seeking to control the narrative and shape public perception.

One of the key features of Trump's gaslighting tactics was his repeated denial of facts or events that contradicted his preferred narrative. Whether it was denying the severity of the COVID-19 pandemic, disputing the results of the 2020 presidential election, or downplaying his administration's failures, Trump consistently sought to distort reality to fit his agenda.

Moreover, Trump's gaslighting tactics were often accompanied by efforts to undermine the credibility of sources that contradicted his version of events, such as the media, scientific experts, or government agencies. By casting doubt on the motives and competence of these sources, Trump sought to discredit their findings and reinforce his narrative, further confusing the public and undermining their ability to discern truth from falsehood.

Furthermore, Trump's gaslighting tactics had far-reaching consequences for public discourse and democratic norms. By distorting reality and blurring the lines between fact and fiction, Trump undermined the integrity of public discourse and eroded public trust in the institutions essential for democratic governance.

Overall, Trump's use of gaslighting tactics to distort reality and manipulate public perception was a dangerous assault on the foundations of democracy. By blurring the lines between reality and falsehood and undermining public trust in objective truth, Trump sought to control the narrative and shape public perception to his advantage, ultimately posing a significant threat to the integrity of democratic governance.

Weaponizing Fear and Division

Trump's fake news strategy frequently revolved around weaponizing fear and division among the electorate. He strategically promoted narratives that portrayed immigrants, minorities, and political opponents as existential threats, appealing to the emotions of his supporters and fostering a sense of us-versus-them mentality. This tactic fueled social polarization, distracted from systemic issues, and undermined efforts to promote unity and inclusivity.

One of the critical aspects of Trump's strategy was his use of inflammatory rhetoric and fear-mongering to rally his base and demonize perceived adversaries. Whether through speeches, rallies, or social media posts, Trump consistently portrayed immigrants as criminals and terrorists, minorities as threats to American values, and political opponents as enemies of the people. By tapping into deep-seated fears and prejudices, Trump sought to mobilize his supporters and consolidate power through division.

Moreover, Trump's weaponization of fear and division was often accompanied by efforts to dehumanize and scapegoat marginalized groups, such as immigrants and refugees. By portraying these groups as dangerous and undesirable, Trump sought to justify harsh policies and crackdowns on immigration while deflecting attention from his administration's failures and shortcomings.

Furthermore, Trump's strategy of stoking fear and division had far-reaching consequences for social cohesion and democratic norms. By fostering a climate of fear and mistrust, Trump undermined efforts to promote unity and inclusivity and fueled social polarization that hindered constructive dialogue and collaboration across political lines.

Overall, Trump's fake news strategy of weaponizing fear and division was a calculated attempt to consolidate power and maintain political support. By promoting narratives that demonized immigrants, minorities, and political opponents, Trump appealed to the emotions of his supporters and fostered a sense of us-versus-them mentality that undermined efforts to promote unity and inclusivity in American society.

Lack of Accountability

Trump's persistent use of fake news tactics had a profound impact on accountability, as it undermined efforts to hold him responsible for his words and actions. By consistently labeling any criticism or scrutiny of his actions as partisan or biased, Trump created a narrative wherein he portrayed himself as a victim of media persecution, effectively inoculating himself against accountability and weakening democratic norms.

One of the critical aspects of Trump's strategy was his relentless attacks on the media as "fake news" and "the enemy of the people," which served to delegitimize critical reporting and reinforce his narrative of victimization. By framing himself as a victim of media bias and persecution, Trump sought to deflect attention from his shortcomings and wrongdoing, effectively shielding himself from accountability for his words and actions.

Moreover, Trump's lack of accountability was facilitated by his mastery of social media and his ability to communicate directly with his supporters. Through tweets and other social media posts, Trump could bypass traditional media channels and disseminate his message directly to his followers, reinforcing his narrative and maintaining political support despite negative coverage in the mainstream media.

Furthermore, Trump's lack of accountability had far-reaching consequences for democratic governance, as it hindered efforts to hold elected officials responsible for their conduct and undermined the integrity of public discourse.

By undermining accountability and promoting a narrative of victimization, Trump weakened democratic norms and eroded public trust in the institutions essential for holding elected officials accountable.

Overall, Trump's consistent use of fake news tactics to undermine accountability had a chilling effect on democratic governance, as it effectively shielded him from criticism and scrutiny, hindering efforts to hold him responsible for his words and actions. By framing himself as a victim of media persecution, Trump undermined democratic norms and weakened the integrity of public discourse, posing a significant threat to the health of American democracy.

Normalization of Disinformation

Trump's persistent use of fake news contributed to the normalization of disinformation in public discourse, marking one of the most enduring impacts of his presidency. Through repeated dissemination of falsehoods and misleading narratives, Trump played a significant role in fostering a culture where truth became subjective and facts were treated as optional. This normalization of disinformation has far-reaching consequences for democracy, eroding the foundation of informed decision-making and undermining trust in democratic institutions.

One of the critical aspects of Trump's strategy was his relentless repetition of false or misleading claims, reinforcing his preferred narratives and discrediting contrary evidence. Whether through speeches, interviews, or social media posts, Trump consistently promoted narratives aligned with his agenda, regardless of their accuracy or veracity. Over time, this repetition helped embed these falsehoods into public discourse, making them seem more credible and legitimate to some population segments.

Moreover, Trump's normalization of disinformation was facilitated by his attacks on the media as "fake news" and "the enemy of the people," which served to delegitimize critical reporting and reinforce his narrative of victimization. By undermining the credibility of mainstream media outlets, Trump created a vacuum in which alternative sources of information, including conspiracy theories and partisan propaganda, could flourish, further blurring the lines between truth and fiction.

Furthermore, Trump's normalization of disinformation has far-reaching consequences for democracy, as it undermines the foundation of informed decision-making and erodes trust in democratic institutions. In a society where truth is subjective and facts are treated as optional, citizens are less able to make informed choices about their leaders and policies, weakening the functioning of democratic governance and threatening the integrity of the democratic process.

Overall, Trump's use of fake news contributed to the normalization of disinformation in public discourse, with far-reaching consequences for democracy. By undermining the credibility of mainstream media outlets and promoting falsehoods and misleading narratives, Trump eroded the foundation of informed decision-making and undermined trust in democratic institutions, posing a significant threat to the health of American democracy.

Erosion of Objective Reality

Trump's consistent dissemination of false information played a significant role in the erosion of objective reality in public discourse, contributing to a post-truth environment where facts became increasingly subjective and open to interpretation. This erosion undermined the foundation of rational debate and critical thinking, making it difficult for citizens to make informed decisions based on evidence and reason.

One of the critical aspects of Trump's strategy was his relentless repetition of false or misleading claims, which served to blur the lines between truth and fiction. Whether through speeches, interviews, or social media posts, Trump consistently promoted narratives aligned with his agenda, regardless of their accuracy or veracity. Over time, this repetition helped embed these falsehoods into public discourse, making them seem more credible and legitimate to some population segments.

Moreover, Trump's erosion of objective reality was facilitated by his attacks on the media as "fake news" and "the enemy of the people," which served to delegitimize critical reporting and reinforce his narrative of victimization. By undermining the credibility of mainstream media outlets, Trump created a vacuum in which alternative sources of information, including conspiracy theories and partisan propaganda, could flourish, further blurring the lines between truth and fiction.

Furthermore, Trump's erosion of objective reality has far-reaching consequences for democracy, undermining the foundation of rational debate and critical thinking. In a post-truth environment where facts are treated as optional and subjective, citizens are less able to make informed decisions about their leaders and policies, weakening the functioning of democratic governance and threatening the integrity of the democratic process.

Overall, Trump's persistent dissemination of false information contributed to the erosion of objective reality in public discourse, with far-reaching consequences for democracy. By blurring the lines between truth and fiction and undermining the credibility of mainstream media outlets, Trump made it difficult for citizens to make informed decisions based on evidence and reason, posing a significant threat to the health of American democracy.

Undermining Democratic Institutions

Trump's relentless attacks on the media and other democratic institutions had a profound impact on their ability to serve as watchdogs and checks on executive power, ultimately undermining the mechanisms of accountability that are essential for a healthy democracy. By consistently undermining public trust in these institutions, Trump weakened their ability to hold elected officials accountable and eroded the democratic norms and principles upon which the American system of government is built.

One of the critical aspects of Trump's strategy was his relentless attacks on the media as "fake news" and "the enemy of the people," which served to delegitimize critical reporting and reinforce his narrative of victimization. By portraying the media as biased and untrustworthy, Trump undermined their credibility as independent arbiters of truth and fostered a climate of distrust that made it difficult for citizens to discern fact from fiction.

Moreover, Trump's attacks on other democratic institutions, such as the judiciary, intelligence agencies, and scientific experts, further eroded public trust in these institutions and weakened their ability to serve as adequate checks on executive power. By casting doubt on the motives and competence of these institutions, Trump undermined their credibility and effectiveness, hindering their ability to hold elected officials accountable and uphold the rule of law.

Furthermore, Trump's erosion of public trust in democratic institutions had far-reaching consequences for the separation of powers and the rule of law. By weakening the mechanisms of accountability that are essential for a healthy democracy, Trump undermined the checks and balances that are designed to prevent abuses of power and protect individual rights and freedoms.

Overall, Trump's attacks on the media and other democratic institutions posed a significant threat to the rule of law and the separation of powers. By undermining public trust in these institutions and weakening their ability to serve as adequate checks on executive power, Trump eroded the democratic norms and principles upon which the American system of government is built, posing a grave danger to the health of American democracy.

Cultivation of Cult-Like Loyalty

Trump's use of fake news tactics played a significant role in cultivating a cult-like loyalty among his supporters, fostering a sense of allegiance that insulated him from criticism and accountability within the Republican Party. By promoting a narrative of victimhood and persecution, Trump effectively positioned himself as a champion of truth against a biased and corrupt establishment, further entrenching his power and influence.

One of the critical aspects of Trump's strategy was his relentless attacks on the media as "fake news" and "the enemy of the people," which served to delegitimize critical reporting and reinforce his narrative of victimization. By portraying himself as a victim of media bias and persecution, Trump cultivated a sense of solidarity among his supporters, who viewed themselves as defenders of truth against a hostile and dishonest establishment.

Moreover, Trump's cultivation of cult-like loyalty was facilitated by his mastery of social media and ability to communicate directly with his supporters. Through tweets and other social media posts, Trump could bypass traditional media channels and disseminate his message directly to his followers, reinforcing his narrative and maintaining political support despite negative coverage in the mainstream media.

Furthermore, Trump's cultivation of a cult-like loyalty had far-reaching consequences for the Republican Party and American democracy. By fostering a sense of allegiance among his supporters, Trump could insulate himself from criticism and accountability within the party, further entrenching his power and influence. This cult-like loyalty also hindered efforts to promote unity and inclusivity within the party, contributing to social polarization and division.

Overall, Trump's use of fake news tactics contributed to the cultivation of a cult-like loyalty among his supporters, fostering a sense of allegiance that insulated him from criticism and accountability within the Republican Party. By promoting a narrative of victimhood and persecution, Trump further entrenches his power and influence, posing a significant challenge to the health of American democracy.

Normalization of Authoritarian Tactics

Trump's embrace of fake news tactics had a significant impact on the normalization of authoritarian tactics such as propaganda, censorship, and the suppression of dissent. By attacking the media as the "enemy of the people" and dismissing unfavorable coverage as fake news, he undermined press freedom and marginalized voices of opposition, ultimately posing a threat to democracy and the principles of free speech and open debate.

One of the critical aspects of Trump's strategy was his relentless attacks on the media as "fake news" and "the enemy of the people," which served to delegitimize critical reporting and reinforce his narrative of victimization. By portraying the media as biased and untrustworthy, Trump undermined their credibility as independent arbiters of truth and fostered a climate of distrust that made it difficult for citizens to discern fact from fiction.

Moreover, Trump's normalization of authoritarian tactics was facilitated by his attempts to silence dissent and suppress criticism within his administration and the broader public. By firing officials who disagreed with him, retaliating against whistleblowers, and threatening legal action against journalists and media outlets, Trump sought to intimidate his opponents and stifle dissent, further undermining democratic norms and principles.

Furthermore, Trump's normalization of authoritarian tactics had far-reaching consequences for democracy and the principles of free speech and open debate. By attacking the media and dismissing unfavorable coverage as fake news, Trump undermined press freedom and marginalized voices of opposition, ultimately eroding the foundations of democratic governance and threatening the integrity of the democratic process.

Overall, Trump's embrace of fake news tactics contributed to the normalization of authoritarian tactics such as propaganda, censorship, and the suppression of dissent, posing a significant threat to democracy and the principles of free speech and open debate. By undermining press freedom and marginalizing voices of opposition, Trump undermined the foundations of democratic governance and weakened the integrity of the democratic process, ultimately posing a grave danger to the health of American democracy.

Legacy of Division and Polarization

Trump's use of fake news tactics exacerbated existing divisions within American society. It deepened polarization along partisan lines, leaving behind a legacy of division and polarization that continues to shape American politics long after his presidency. By promoting conspiracy theories and false narratives, Trump further divided an already fractured electorate and undermined efforts to bridge the partisan divide, posing significant challenges to national unity and democratic governance.

One of the critical aspects of Trump's strategy was his relentless attacks on the media as "fake news" and "the enemy of the people," which served to delegitimize critical reporting and reinforce his narrative of victimization. By portraying the media as biased and untrustworthy, Trump undermined their credibility as independent arbiters of truth and fostered a climate of distrust that made it difficult for citizens to discern fact from fiction.

Moreover, Trump's promotion of conspiracy theories and false narratives fueled social polarization by reinforcing existing partisan divides and deepening distrust between political factions. By amplifying fringe beliefs and legitimizing extremist views, Trump contributed to a toxic political climate characterized by tribalism, distrust, and hatred.

Furthermore, Trump's legacy of division and polarization has far-reaching consequences for American democracy and governance. By exacerbating partisan divisions and deepening polarization, Trump undermined efforts to find common ground and compromise on important issues, hindering the functioning of democratic institutions and impeding progress on critical policy challenges.

Overall, Trump's use of fake news tactics left behind a legacy of division and polarization that continues to shape American politics long after his presidency. By promoting conspiracy theories and false narratives, Trump exacerbated existing divisions within American society and deepened polarization along partisan lines, posing significant challenges to national unity and democratic governance.

Impact on Public Discourse

Trump's use of fake news had a profound impact on public discourse, reshaping the landscape of political conversation and shifting the focus away from substantive issues toward sensationalized narratives. By promoting falsehoods and conspiracy theories, he distorted public perception. He diverted attention from pressing issues such as healthcare, climate change, and economic inequality, ultimately hindering efforts to address the nation's complex challenges and undermining the quality of democratic deliberation.

One of the critical aspects of Trump's strategy was his relentless attacks on the media as "fake news" and "the enemy of the people," which served to delegitimize critical reporting and reinforce his narrative of victimization. By framing the media as biased and untrustworthy, Trump undermined their role as gatekeepers of information and fostered a climate of distrust that made it difficult for citizens to discern fact from fiction.

Moreover, Trump's promotion of falsehoods and conspiracy theories sensationalized public discourse, capturing the media's attention and dominating the news cycle with sensationalized narratives. By amplifying fringe beliefs and legitimizing extremist views, Trump contributed to a toxic political climate characterized by polarization, distrust, and hatred.

Furthermore, Trump's distortion of public discourse had far-reaching consequences for democratic governance and civic engagement. By diverting attention from substantive issues and promoting sensationalized narratives, Trump hindered efforts to address pressing challenges facing the nation and undermined the quality of democratic deliberation, making it difficult for citizens to engage in informed decision-making and hold elected officials accountable.

Overall, Trump's use of fake news profoundly impacted public discourse, shifting the focus away from substantive issues toward sensationalized narratives and distorting public perception. By promoting falsehoods and conspiracy theories, Trump undermined efforts to address complex challenges facing the nation and hindered the quality of democratic deliberation, posing significant challenges to the health of American democracy.

Global Consequences

Trump's dissemination of fake news had ripple effects beyond the borders of the United States, influencing public opinion and political discourse worldwide with significant global consequences. His attacks on the media and promotion of conspiracy theories undermined press freedom and democratic norms in other countries, encouraging authoritarian leaders and weakening efforts to promote democracy and human rights globally. This global impact underscores the interconnected nature of disinformation and highlights the need for international cooperation to combat its spread.

One of the critical aspects of Trump's strategy was his relentless attacks on the media as "fake news" and "the enemy of the people," which served to delegitimize critical reporting and reinforce his narrative of victimization. By undermining the media's credibility, Trump contributed to a global climate of distrust in journalistic institutions, making it more difficult for citizens worldwide to access accurate and reliable information.

Moreover, Trump's promotion of conspiracy theories and falsehoods had a destabilizing effect on global politics, fueling social polarization and undermining democratic norms in other countries. By amplifying fringe beliefs and legitimizing extremist views, Trump encouraged authoritarian leaders and weakened efforts to promote democracy and human rights globally, posing a significant challenge to the advancement of freedom and democracy worldwide.

Furthermore, Trump's dissemination of fake news had far-reaching consequences for international relations and diplomatic efforts. By promoting falsehoods and conspiracy theories, Trump undermined efforts to build trust and cooperation between nations, making it more difficult to address shared challenges such as climate change, terrorism, and global health crises.

Overall, Trump's dissemination of fake news had ripple effects beyond the borders of the United States, influencing public opinion and political discourse worldwide with significant global consequences. By attacking the media and promoting conspiracy theories, Trump undermined press freedom and democratic norms in other countries, encouraging authoritarian leaders and weakening efforts to promote democracy and human rights globally, underscoring the interconnected nature of disinformation and highlighting the need for international cooperation to combat its spread.

Normalization of Lying

Trump's frequent use of falsehoods and lies profoundly impacted the normalization of lying in public life, contributing to a climate where the truth became increasingly subjective and open to interpretation. By repeatedly making false statements and refusing to retract or correct them, he undermined the value of truth and honesty in political discourse, eroding public trust in elected officials and institutions and weakening the foundations of democracy and civic engagement.

One of the critical aspects of Trump's strategy was his unapologetic disregard for the truth, demonstrated by his persistent dissemination of falsehoods and lies. Whether through speeches, interviews, or social media posts, Trump consistently promoted narratives aligned with his agenda, regardless of their accuracy or veracity. Over time, this normalization of lying helped to blur the lines between fact and fiction, making it increasingly difficult for citizens to discern truth from falsehood.

Moreover, Trump's normalization of lying was facilitated by his attacks on the media as "fake news" and "the enemy of the people," which served to delegitimize critical reporting and reinforce his narrative of victimization. By framing the media as biased and untrustworthy, Trump undermined their role as gatekeepers of information and fostered a climate of distrust that made it difficult for citizens to discern fact from fiction.

Furthermore, Trump's normalization of lying had far-reaching consequences for democratic governance and civic engagement. By eroding public trust in elected officials and institutions, Trump undermined the foundations of democracy and civic engagement, making it more difficult for citizens to engage in informed decision-making and hold their leaders accountable.

Overall, Trump's frequent use of falsehoods and lies contributed to normalizing lying in public life, eroding public trust in elected officials and institutions and further weakening the foundations of democracy and civic engagement. By undermining the value of truth and honesty in political discourse, Trump paved the way for a climate where the truth became increasingly subjective and open to interpretation, posing significant challenges to the health of American democracy.

Manipulation of Public Opinion

Trump's use of fake news was a deliberate strategy aimed at manipulating public opinion and consolidating his power. By selectively disseminating information and attacking dissenting voices, he sought to control the narrative and shape public perception to his advantage. This manipulation of public opinion undermined the democratic principle of informed consent, where citizens make decisions based on accurate and reliable information.

One of the critical aspects of Trump's strategy was his relentless attacks on the media as "fake news" and "the enemy of the people," which served to delegitimize critical reporting and reinforce his narrative of victimization. By portraying the media as biased and untrustworthy, Trump undermined their role as independent arbiters of truth and fostered a climate of distrust that made it difficult for citizens to discern fact from fiction.

Moreover, Trump's manipulation of public opinion was facilitated by his mastery of social media and ability to communicate directly with his supporters. Through tweets and other social media posts, Trump could bypass traditional media channels and disseminate his message directly to his followers, reinforcing his narrative and maintaining political support despite negative coverage in the mainstream media.

Furthermore, Trump's manipulation of public opinion had far-reaching consequences for democratic governance and civic engagement. By shaping the narrative and controlling the flow of information, Trump undermined the democratic principle of informed consent, where citizens make decisions based on accurate and reliable information. Instead, he sought to manipulate public opinion to his advantage, consolidating his power and undermining the integrity of the democratic process.

Overall, Trump's use of fake news was a deliberate strategy aimed at manipulating public opinion and maintaining his grip on power. By shaping the narrative and controlling the flow of information, he sought to control public perception and undermine the democratic principle of informed consent, posing significant challenges to the health of American democracy.

Challenges for Future Administrations

Trump's legacy of using fake news poses significant challenges for future administrations and democratic governance. The erosion of trust in media, institutions, and objective reality will require concerted efforts to rebuild and restore faith in democratic norms and principles. Addressing the proliferation of fake news will require a multi-faceted approach, including media literacy education, regulatory reforms, and efforts to promote transparency and accountability in government.

One of the critical challenges for future administrations will be rebuilding trust in media and institutions that have been undermined by Trump's attacks on the press and promotion of fake news. Restoring confidence in the media will require transparency, accountability, and a commitment to truth-telling and efforts to counter disinformation and promote media literacy among the public.

Moreover, future administrations must address the proliferation of fake news and misinformation online, exacerbated by Trump's use of social media to disseminate false or misleading information. This will require regulatory reforms to hold social media platforms accountable for the spread of misinformation, as well as efforts to promote media literacy and critical thinking skills among users.

Furthermore, future administrations will need to promote transparency and accountability in government to rebuild public trust and confidence in democratic institutions. This will require a commitment to open and honest communication and efforts to hold elected officials and government agencies accountable for their actions.

Addressing the challenges posed by Trump's legacy of using fake news will require a comprehensive and multi-faceted approach that addresses the root causes of disinformation and promotes transparency, accountability, and media literacy in government and society. By rebuilding trust in media, institutions, and objective reality, future administrations can work to strengthen democratic governance and uphold the principles of democracy for generations to come.

Erosion of Trust in Experts

Trump's frequent dismissal of expert opinion and scientific consensus profoundly impacted the erosion of trust in authoritative sources of information, further undermining public confidence in experts and institutions that rely on evidence-based decision-making. By casting doubt on facts and promoting alternative narratives, he contributed to a climate of skepticism and distrust that hindered efforts to address pressing issues such as public health crises, environmental challenges, and national security threats.

One of the critical aspects of Trump's strategy was his consistent rejection of expert opinion and scientific consensus on a wide range of issues, from climate change to public health. By dismissing facts and promoting alternative narratives aligned with his agenda, Trump undermined the credibility of experts and institutions relying on evidence-based decision-making, such as government agencies, scientific organizations, and academic institutions.

Moreover, Trump's attacks on experts and institutions were often accompanied by efforts to promote alternative narratives that downplayed the severity of pressing issues or advanced his political interests. For example, despite overwhelming scientific evidence to the contrary, he frequently downplayed the threat of climate change. He promoted unproven remedies for public health crises such as COVID-19, effectively undermining efforts to address these challenges.

Furthermore, Trump's erosion of trust in experts had far-reaching consequences for public policy and governance, making it more difficult to address pressing issues such as public health crises, environmental challenges, and national security threats. Trump hindered efforts to implement evidence-based policies and solutions for addressing society's complex challenges by undermining public confidence in experts and scientific consensus.

Overall, Trump's frequent dismissal of expert opinion and scientific consensus contributed to the erosion of trust in authoritative sources of information, further undermining public confidence in experts and institutions that rely on evidence-based decision-making. This erosion of trust hindered efforts to address pressing issues such as public health crises, environmental challenges, and national security threats, highlighting the need for a renewed commitment to evidence-based policymaking and the restoration of trust in experts and authoritative sources of information.

Normalization of Personal Attacks

In the grand puzzle of political discourse, one piece that became glaringly prominent during Trump's tenure was the normalization of personal attacks. Trump, like a savvy puzzle master, often employed tactics that veered from constructive criticism to direct assaults on individuals who dared to oppose him or his administration. His weapon of choice? Fake news.

Trump's strategy was akin to forcefully fitting a mismatched puzzle piece into the larger picture, resorting to ad hominem attacks and character assassination against his critics. Instead of engaging with their arguments or addressing the issues, he opted for the low road, aiming to discredit his opponents and erode their credibility.

Picture this puzzle - with each personal attack, Trump sought not only to silence dissent but also to solidify his position as the unrivaled solver of America's problems. By casting doubt on the character and integrity of those who challenged him, he attempted to paint himself as the lone voice of reason in a sea of falsehoods.

The consequence of this normalization of personal attacks was profound. In the puzzle of political discourse, it introduced a corrosive element that tainted the overall picture. The once civil and reasoned debates led to a toxic environment where insults and smear tactics became par for the course.

As each piece of the puzzle fell into place, the coarsening of political rhetoric became evident. Like rough edges on a puzzle piece, personal attacks left their mark, chipping away at the essence of democratic debate. Rather than fostering meaningful dialogue and exchanging ideas, the discourse descended into a battle of insults and mudslinging.

Ultimately, the normalization of personal attacks under Trump's leadership diminished the quality of democratic debate. It was as if a vital puzzle piece had been misplaced, leaving the picture incomplete and fragmented. Without respectful discourse and genuine engagement, the puzzle of democracy became increasingly challenging.

Exploitation of Social Media Algorithms

In the intricate puzzle of modern communication, Trump emerged as a master manipulator, deftly exploiting the algorithms of social media platforms to his advantage. With each post, tweet, and share, he strategically maneuvered his message through the digital landscape, leveraging the power of algorithms to amplify his voice and extend his reach far beyond traditional boundaries.

Imagine the puzzle of social media algorithms as a complex web, where each interaction serves as a thread connecting users to content. Like a skilled puzzle solver, Trump understood this web's mechanics and utilized it to his advantage. By feeding the algorithms with provocative and attention-grabbing content, he ensured that his messages would gain traction and visibility.

In this digital puzzle, Trump's mastery lay in his ability to bypass traditional gatekeepers and speak directly to his audience. Through social media platforms, he could disseminate true and false information to millions of followers with just a few clicks. The viral nature of social media ensured that his messages spread rapidly, amplifying his influence and shaping public opinion.

However, as each piece of the puzzle fell into place, the darker side of Trump's exploitation of social media algorithms became apparent. The very mechanisms that enabled his message to reach a broad audience also facilitated the spread of fake news and misinformation. Like a virus spreading through the puzzle, false narratives and misleading information proliferated, eroding trust and sowing user confusion.

This exploitation of social media algorithms exacerbated existing challenges related to online disinformation. In the puzzle of digital communication, Trump's actions acted as a catalyst, fueling the fire of misinformation and undermining efforts to combat it. As falsehoods spread unchecked, the integrity of online discourse was questioned, further complicating the puzzle of truth in the digital age.

Ultimately, Trump's strategic use of social media algorithms reshaped the landscape of political communication. In the puzzle of democracy, his tactics introduced a new set of challenges, highlighting the need for greater transparency and accountability in the digital realm. As society grapples with the implications of his actions, the puzzle of social media algorithms remains a complex and evolving puzzle, with far-reaching implications for the future of democracy.

Legacy of Skepticism and Cynicism

In the intricate puzzle of American politics, Trump's tenure left behind a lasting legacy characterized by skepticism and cynicism. Like pieces of a puzzle that don't quite fit, his relentless attacks on the media and propagation of fake news reshaped the landscape of public perception, leaving a climate of distrust and suspicion.

Imagine the puzzle of public trust as a fragile construction built upon the foundation of credibility and transparency. Trump, like a puzzle disruptor, systematically dismantled this foundation, casting doubt on the integrity of the media and labeling any unfavorable coverage as "fake news." He chipped away at the trust that once bound the American public to their institutions with each accusation and inflammatory tweet.

In this puzzle of perception, Trump's rhetoric fostered a culture of skepticism and cynicism, where truth became subjective, and facts were up for debate. By sowing seeds of doubt and suspicion, he undermined efforts to promote civic engagement and democratic participation. Instead of actively participating in the puzzle of democracy, many Americans withdrew, disillusioned by the perceived manipulation and deceit.

As each piece of the puzzle fell into place, the consequences of Trump's legacy became increasingly apparent. The once-solid foundation of trust crumbled, leaving behind a fractured landscape where conspiracy theories and misinformation thrived. In this environment, the puzzle of democracy became increasingly challenging, with skepticism and cynicism casting a shadow over every decision and action.

The legacy of skepticism and cynicism poses significant challenges for rebuilding trust in institutions and fostering a culture of informed citizenship. Like a puzzle missing key pieces, restoring faith in the media and democratic processes requires a concerted effort to address the underlying issues that Trump's rhetoric exposed. It requires transparency, accountability, and a commitment to truth, even when inconvenient.

In the puzzle of American democracy, Trump's legacy serves as a cautionary tale, reminding us of the fragility of trust and the importance of preserving it. As society grapples with the implications of his actions, the puzzle of rebuilding trust becomes paramount, requiring collaboration and collective effort to create a more resilient foundation for the future.

Long-Term Implications for Democracy

In the grand puzzle of democracy, Trump's utilization of fake news has left a lasting imprint with far-reaching implications, reshaping the landscape of governance both domestically and globally. His tactics, like misplaced puzzle pieces, disrupted the delicate balance of democratic norms and institutions, fostering polarization and eroding trust in objective reality.

Imagine the puzzle of democracy as a complex structure built upon transparency, accountability, and civic engagement principles. Trump, with his arsenal of fake news, systematically weakened these foundations, casting doubt on the legitimacy of democratic institutions and sowing seeds of division among the populace.

In this puzzle of governance, Trump's tactics fueled polarization, deepening existing divides and creating new fault lines within society. As pieces pushed to opposite ends of the puzzle, Americans became increasingly entrenched in echo chambers, where differing perspectives were dismissed as partisan propaganda rather than legitimate points of view.

As each piece of the puzzle fell into place, the long-term implications of Trump's actions became apparent. The erosion of trust in objective reality undermined the very essence of democratic governance, where informed decision-making relies on a shared understanding of facts and evidence. In this environment of doubt and uncertainty, the puzzle of democracy became increasingly challenging, with no clear path forward.

The enduring legacy of Trump's fake news tactics serves as a stark reminder of the fragility of democracy in the digital age. In the governance puzzle, disinformation acts as a corrosive force, eating away at the pillars of democracy and leaving behind a fractured landscape of distrust and division.

Addressing the root causes of disinformation and rebuilding trust in democratic institutions and values is paramount to safeguarding the future of democracy. Like fitting together the puzzle pieces, it requires collective effort and a commitment to upholding the principles underpinning democratic governance.

As society grapples with the long-term implications of Trump's actions, the puzzle of democracy remains a work in progress, with the fate of democratic governance hanging in the balance. Only by confronting the challenges posed by fake news and reaffirming our commitment to truth and transparency can we hope to piece together a more resilient and inclusive democracy for future generations.

Normalization of Conspiracy Theories

In the intricate puzzle of public discourse, Trump's presidency witnessed the normalization of conspiracy theories, reshaping the landscape of information dissemination and public perception. Using fake news and promoting baseless claims, he blurred the line between fact and fiction, leaving a trail of confusion and distrust in his wake.

Imagine the puzzle of truth as a fragile construction built upon a foundation of evidence and rational inquiry. Like a puzzle disruptor, Trump introduced a new set of pieces that didn't quite fit, crediting conspiracy theories and unsubstantiated rumors. With each endorsement, he eroded public trust in established information sources and undermined the notion of objective reality.

In this perception puzzle, Trump's promotion of conspiracy theories contributed to paranoia and distrust, where every piece of information was viewed with suspicion. Like puzzle pieces scattered haphazardly, Americans grappled with competing narratives, unsure what to believe or whom to trust.

As each piece of the puzzle fell into place, the consequences of Trump's normalization of conspiracy theories became increasingly apparent. The once-clear lines between fact and fiction blurred, leaving a fractured landscape of competing truths. In this environment of uncertainty, the puzzle of public discourse became increasingly challenging to solve, with no consensus on which pieces belonged where.

The normalization of conspiracy theories further divided society along ideological lines, exacerbating existing fractures and deepening mistrust between individuals and groups. As puzzle pieces were pushed to opposite ends, Americans became increasingly isolated within echo chambers, where dissenting voices were dismissed as heresy rather than legitimate points of view.

Addressing the normalization of conspiracy theories requires a concerted effort to reaffirm the importance of evidence-based reasoning and critical thinking. Like fitting together the puzzle pieces, it requires collaboration and dialogue to bridge the gaps that divide us and restore trust in established sources of information.

As society grapples with the long-term implications of Trump's normalization of conspiracy theories, the puzzle of public discourse remains in flux, with the truth obscured by a cloud of uncertainty. We hope to piece together a more coherent and inclusive understanding of reality by confronting the challenges posed by misinformation and reaffirming our commitment to rational inquiry.

Undermining Democratic Institutions

In the intricate puzzle of democracy, Trump's presidency witnessed a concerted effort to undermine the very institutions that form the backbone of democratic governance. His attacks extended beyond the media to encompass vital pillars such as the judiciary, electoral process, and law enforcement agencies. Like a puzzle master wielding a sledgehammer, Trump sought to dismantle the foundations of democracy, casting doubt on their legitimacy and integrity.

Imagine the puzzle of democratic institutions as a sturdy structure built upon the principles of fairness, accountability, and the rule of law. Like a puzzle disruptor, Trump chipped away at this structure, questioning the legitimacy of institutions designed to safeguard citizens' rights and freedoms. With each attack, he undermined public confidence in the democratic process, leaving a landscape of doubt and uncertainty.

In this puzzle of governance, Trump's assaults on democratic institutions posed a significant threat to the stability and legitimacy of the political system. By casting doubt on the judiciary, he called into question the impartiality of the courts. He eroded trust in the rule of law. By questioning the integrity of the electoral process, he undermined confidence in the democratic process itself, sowing seeds of doubt about the legitimacy of election outcomes.

As each piece of the puzzle fell into place, the consequences of Trump's actions became increasingly apparent. The erosion of trust in democratic institutions created a climate of political instability and uncertainty, where the very foundations of democracy were called into question. In this environment of doubt and distrust, the governance puzzle became increasingly difficult to solve, with no clear path forward.

Addressing the undermining of democratic institutions requires a concerted effort to reaffirm the importance of upholding the principles of democracy and the rule of law. Like fitting together the puzzle pieces, it requires a commitment to transparency, accountability, and respect for the institutions that safeguard our rights and freedoms.

As society grapples with the long-term implications of Trump's attacks on democratic institutions, the puzzle of governance remains in flux, with the stability and legitimacy of the political system hanging in the balance. Only by confronting the challenges posed by these attacks and reaffirming our commitment to democratic values can we hope to rebuild trust and ensure the resilience of our democratic institutions for future generations.

Polarization of the Information Ecosystem

In the intricate puzzle of the information ecosystem, Trump's utilization of fake news acted as a catalyst, exacerbating existing divisions and deepening societal polarization. His strategic messaging targeted specific demographic groups, amplifying partisan narratives and reinforcing pre-existing beliefs and biases. As puzzle pieces were pushed to opposite ends, individuals became increasingly isolated within echo chambers, where dissenting views were dismissed and alternative perspectives were scarce.

Imagine the puzzle of the information ecosystem as a vast landscape where information streams flow freely, shaping public opinion and influencing decision-making. Like a puzzle disruptor, Trump manipulated these streams, channeling his messaging to cater to the preferences and biases of specific audiences. Through targeted messaging and selective amplification, he intensified polarization, further fragmenting the puzzle of public discourse.

In this puzzle of perception, Trump's use of fake news deepened societal divisions, hindering efforts to promote mutual understanding and compromise. By reinforcing partisan narratives and amplifying ideological differences, he created a climate where dialogue and consensus-building became increasingly challenging. Like puzzle pieces that refuse to fit together, Americans were entrenched in ideological bubbles, where conflicting perspectives were viewed as threats rather than growth opportunities.

As each piece of the puzzle fell into place, the consequences of Trump's actions became increasingly apparent. The polarization of the information ecosystem led to a breakdown in communication and a widening gap between opposing viewpoints. In this environment of division and distrust, the puzzle of societal cohesion became increasingly difficult to solve, with no clear path forward.

Addressing the polarization of the information ecosystem requires a concerted effort to promote media literacy, critical thinking, and cross-cultural understanding. It requires dialogue and engagement across ideological lines, like fitting together the puzzle pieces and fostering empathy and mutual respect for differing perspectives.

As society grapples with the long-term implications of Trump's use of fake news, the puzzle of the information ecosystem remains in flux, with the stability and cohesion of society hanging in the balance. We hope to piece together a more cohesive and inclusive society for future generations by confronting the challenges posed by polarization and reaffirming our commitment to open dialogue and mutual understanding.

Legacy of Disinformation

In the puzzle of the political landscape, Trump's legacy of using fake news has left an indelible mark, reshaping public perceptions and attitudes long after his presidency. The normalization of disinformation and the erosion of trust in institutions have created fertile ground for spreading misinformation and conspiracy theories, posing ongoing challenges to democracy and public discourse.

Imagine the legacy of disinformation as a shadow cast over the puzzle of public perception, distorting reality and clouding judgment. Trump, like a puzzle master manipulating the pieces, strategically deployed fake news to sow doubt and confusion among the populace. He blurred the line between fact and fiction through a relentless barrage of misinformation, leaving behind a legacy of skepticism and mistrust.

In this puzzle of perception, Trump's legacy of disinformation continues to shape public discourse, fueling polarization and division. Normalizing falsehoods has created a culture where truth is subjective and facts are up for debate. Like puzzle pieces that refuse to align, Americans grapple with competing narratives, unsure of what to believe or whom to trust.

As each piece of the puzzle falls into place, the consequences of Trump's legacy become increasingly apparent. The erosion of trust in institutions has weakened the foundation of democracy, leaving society vulnerable to the spread of misinformation and conspiracy theories. In this environment of uncertainty, the puzzle of public discourse becomes increasingly difficult to solve, with no clear path forward.

Addressing the legacy of disinformation requires a concerted effort to rebuild trust in institutions and reaffirm the importance of facts and evidence-based reasoning. It requires a commitment to transparency, accountability, and integrity in public discourse, such as fitting together the puzzle pieces.

As society grapples with the ongoing challenges posed by Trump's legacy of disinformation, the puzzle of democracy remains in flux, with the future of public discourse hanging in the balance. Only by confronting the root causes of disinformation and reaffirming our commitment to truth and transparency can we hope to piece together a more resilient and inclusive democracy for future generations.

Lessons Learned

In the aftermath of Trump's presidency, his use of fake news stands as a cautionary tale, highlighting the dangers of weaponizing misinformation for political gain. It serves as a stark reminder of the fragility of truth in the digital age. It underscores the importance of vigilance in defending against disinformation.

Imagine the lessons learned from Trump's use of fake news as pieces of wisdom scattered across the puzzle of public discourse. He strategically manipulated information and exploited vulnerabilities in the information ecosystem, undermining trust and sowing division. The consequences of his actions reverberate throughout society, leaving behind a legacy of skepticism and mistrust.

In this perception puzzle, the lessons learned from Trump's presidency emphasize the importance of promoting media literacy and upholding the principles of truth and transparency in democratic governance. By arming individuals with the tools to discern fact from fiction, society can build a more resilient defense against the spread of misinformation.

As each lesson is internalized and applied, the puzzle of public discourse begins to take shape, with truth and integrity at its core. By learning from past mistakes, societies can better equip themselves to confront the challenges posed by fake news and safeguard the integrity of democratic institutions.

Addressing the lessons learned from Trump's use of fake news requires a collective effort to promote media literacy, critical thinking, and civic engagement. Like fitting together the puzzle pieces, it requires a commitment to truth and transparency in all aspects of public discourse.

As society reflects on the lessons learned from Trump's presidency, the puzzle of democracy becomes more evident, with the principles of truth and integrity guiding the way forward. By remaining vigilant in defending against disinformation and upholding the values of democracy, societies can build a more resilient and inclusive future for all.

Manipulation of Public Perception

In the complex puzzle of political strategy, Trump's use of fake news was not merely about spreading false information but also about manipulating public perception and shaping narratives to align with his political agenda. Through selective dissemination of information and strategic messaging, he sought to control the narrative, shape public opinion, and maintain his grip on power. However, this manipulation of public perception came at a significant cost, undermining the democratic principle of informed consent, where citizens make decisions based on accurate and reliable information.

Imagine the manipulation of public perception as a tangled web, carefully woven by Trump and his administration to obscure truth and distort reality. Like a skilled puzzle solver, Trump strategically deployed fake news to advance his agenda, targeting specific audiences and amplifying partisan narratives. Through a combination of misinformation, propaganda, and spin, he created a distorted image of reality that served his interests while eroding trust in established sources of information.

In this puzzle of public perception, Trump's manipulation undermined the democratic principle of informed consent, where citizens rely on accurate and reliable information to make informed decisions. By controlling the narrative and shaping public opinion, he sought to maintain his grip on power and suppress dissenting voices. However, in doing so, he compromised the integrity of the democratic process and weakened the foundations of democracy itself.

As each piece of the puzzle fell into place, the consequences of Trump's manipulation became increasingly apparent. The erosion of trust in institutions and the distortion of reality created confusion and uncertainty, where truth became elusive and facts were subjective. In this environment of manipulation and misinformation, the puzzle of public perception became increasingly difficult to solve, with no clear path forward.

Addressing the manipulation of public perception requires a concerted effort to promote transparency, accountability, and media literacy. Like fitting together the puzzle pieces, it requires a commitment to truth and integrity in all aspects of public discourse. By empowering citizens to evaluate information and hold leaders accountable for their actions critically, societies can safeguard the democratic principle of informed consent and ensure the integrity of the democratic process.

Erosion of Norms of Civility

In the puzzle of political discourse, Trump's use of fake news was accompanied by a troubling trend

the erosion of norms of civility in public life. Through incendiary rhetoric, personal attacks, and inflammatory language, he contributed to a coarsening of political discourse that undermined efforts to promote constructive dialogue and compromise. This erosion of civility exacerbated political polarization and division, leaving a fractured landscape where mutual understanding and cooperation seemed increasingly out of reach.

Imagine the erosion of norms of civility as cracks formed in the puzzle of public discourse, gradually widening as Trump's rhetoric grew more divisive and inflammatory. Like a puzzle solver wielding a hammer, he shattered the conventions of civil discourse, resorting to name-calling, bullying, and character assassination to silence critics and assert dominance. With each attack, the fabric of civility frayed, leaving behind a toxic environment where insults and vitriol replaced reasoned debate.

In this puzzle of political discourse, Trump's actions exacerbated political polarization and division, further entrenching ideological divides and deepening mistrust between individuals and groups. The erosion of civility created a climate where cooperation and compromise became increasingly elusive as adversaries retreated to their respective corners rather than engaging in meaningful dialogue. As puzzle pieces were pushed to opposite ends, Americans isolated themselves within echo chambers, where the cacophony of partisan rhetoric drowned out dissenting voices.

As each piece of the puzzle fell into place, the consequences of Trump's erosion of civility became increasingly apparent. The breakdown of norms of civility undermined the foundations of democratic governance, hindering efforts to address pressing challenges and find common ground. In this environment of hostility and hatred, the puzzle of political cooperation became increasingly difficult to solve, with no clear path forward.

Addressing the erosion of norms of civility requires a concerted effort to promote respect, empathy, and understanding in public discourse. Like fitting together the puzzle pieces, it requires a commitment to civility and decency in all interactions, even when disagreements are profound. By fostering a culture of respect and dialogue, societies can repair the cracks in the puzzle of political discourse and rebuild trust in democratic institutions.

Creation of Parallel Realities

In the complex puzzle of public perception, Trump's use of fake news played a pivotal role in creating parallel realities, where individuals inhabited echo chambers of information that reinforced their beliefs and biases. He fostered a fragmented information landscape by promoting alternative narratives and conspiracy theories where truth became subjective and relative. This fragmentation of reality hindered efforts to promote a shared understanding of the facts. It undermined the possibility of meaningful dialogue and consensus-building.

Imagine the creation of parallel realities as diverging paths in the puzzle of public perception, each leading to a different version of reality. Trump, like a puzzle master manipulating the pieces, strategically promoted alternative narratives and conspiracy theories to cater to the preferences and biases of specific audiences. Through misinformation, propaganda, and spin, he created a distorted image of reality that served his interests while deepening social divisions.

In this puzzle of perception, individuals retreated into echo chambers of information that reinforced their existing beliefs and biases. Like puzzle pieces that refuse to align, Americans were entrenched in ideological bubbles, where dissenting views were dismissed, and alternative perspectives were scarce. The proliferation of fake news and alternative narratives created a fragmented information landscape where truth became elusive, and facts were up for debate.

As each piece of the puzzle fell into place, the consequences of Trump's creation of parallel realities became increasingly apparent. The fragmentation of reality hindered efforts to promote a shared understanding of the facts. It undermined the possibility of meaningful dialogue and consensus-building.

In this environment of division and distrust, the puzzle of public discourse became increasingly difficult to solve, with no clear path forward.

Addressing the creation of parallel realities requires a concerted effort to promote media literacy, critical thinking, and cross-cultural understanding. It requires dialogue and engagement across ideological lines, like fitting together the puzzle pieces and fostering empathy and mutual respect for differing perspectives. By challenging false narratives and promoting a commitment to truth and transparency, societies can bridge the gaps between parallel realities and work toward a more cohesive understanding of the world.

Legacy of Mistrust in Democratic Processes

In the puzzle of democratic governance, Trump's relentless attacks on democratic institutions and processes, such as the electoral system and the peaceful transfer of power, have left a profound and lasting legacy of mistrust among the American public. By sowing doubt in the integrity of democratic processes, he undermined confidence in the political system's legitimacy and the rule of law. This legacy of mistrust challenges efforts to strengthen democratic governance and uphold democratic values.

Imagine the legacy of mistrust as a dark cloud hanging over the puzzle of democratic processes, casting doubt on the very foundations of the political system. Trump, like a puzzle disruptor, systematically undermined confidence in democratic institutions, questioning the fairness and integrity of elections and casting doubt on the peaceful transfer of power. Through a barrage of baseless claims and inflammatory rhetoric, he eroded public trust in the pillars of democracy, leaving behind a landscape of skepticism and uncertainty.

In this puzzle of democratic governance, Trump's attacks on democratic processes have created a climate of mistrust and skepticism among the American public. The legacy of his actions lingers, casting a shadow over the integrity of elections and the legitimacy of political institutions. The erosion of trust in democratic processes poses ongoing challenges to strengthening democratic governance and upholding democratic values as citizens question the fairness and transparency of the political system.

As each piece of the puzzle falls into place, the consequences of Trump's legacy of mistrust become increasingly apparent. The erosion of confidence in democratic processes hinders efforts to promote civic engagement and participation as citizens become disillusioned with the political system. In this environment of doubt and uncertainty, the puzzle of democratic governance becomes increasingly difficult to solve, with no clear path forward.

Addressing the legacy of mistrust in democratic processes requires a concerted effort to rebuild confidence in the integrity of elections and the fairness of political institutions. Like fitting together the puzzle pieces, it requires transparency, accountability, and a commitment to upholding democratic values. By restoring trust in democratic processes, societies can begin to repair the damage inflicted by Trump's attacks and ensure the resilience of democratic governance for future generations.

Challenges for Rebuilding Trust

In the aftermath of Trump's presidency, his use of fake news has left behind a daunting legacy of distrust and division that will not easily be overcome. Rebuilding trust in institutions, restoring faith in democratic processes, and promoting a culture of truth and transparency will require sustained efforts from policymakers, civil society organizations, and the media. By confronting the root causes of disinformation and promoting accountability and transparency, societies can begin to address the legacy of mistrust left by Trump's presidency.

Imagine the challenges for rebuilding trust as obstacles strewn across the puzzle of public perception, each representing a barrier to restoring faith in democratic institutions and processes. Trump's relentless attacks on the media, the judiciary, and other pillars of democracy have left a profound and lasting impact, undermining confidence in the integrity of the political system and eroding trust in the rule of law.

In this puzzle of distrust, rebuilding trust will require a multifaceted approach that addresses the root causes of disinformation and promotes accountability and transparency in governance. Policymakers must enact measures to strengthen democratic institutions, protect the integrity of elections, and combat the spread of fake news. Civil society organizations must work to promote media literacy, critical thinking, and civic engagement among the public. The media must adhere to rigorous journalistic standards and hold those in power accountable for their actions.

As each puzzle piece falls into place, the challenges for rebuilding trust become increasingly apparent. The legacy of distrust left by Trump's presidency runs deep, casting a shadow over the integrity of democratic governance and hindering efforts to promote civic engagement and participation. In this environment of uncertainty and division, rebuilding trust becomes increasingly complex, with no easy solutions.

Addressing the challenges of rebuilding trust will require a concerted and sustained effort from all sectors of society. By confronting the root causes of disinformation, promoting accountability and transparency, and fostering a culture of truth and integrity, societies can heal the wounds inflicted by Trump's attacks on democracy and rebuild trust in the institutions that form the foundation of democratic governance.

Cultural Shift in Truth Perception

In the puzzle of societal values, Trump's use of fake news has triggered a profound cultural shift in how truth is perceived and valued. Through his relentless dissemination of falsehoods and dismissal of unfavorable information as fake news, he has undermined the notion of objective truth and fostered a climate where subjective beliefs and opinions hold equal weight to factual evidence. This cultural shift in truth perception poses significant challenges for democratic governance and public discourse, eroding the foundation of shared reality upon which informed decision-making relies.

Imagine the cultural shift in truth perception as seismic tremors shake the very foundations of the puzzle of societal values. Trump's repeated dissemination of falsehoods and his attacks on the media as purveyors of fake news has created a climate of uncertainty and doubt, where truth is no longer seen as an objective reality but rather as a matter of personal interpretation. In this environment, facts become malleable, and reality becomes subjective, leaving individuals to construct their version of the truth based on their beliefs and biases.

In this puzzle of truth perception, the erosion of the notion of objective truth poses significant challenges for democratic governance and public discourse. In a society where subjective beliefs hold equal weight to factual evidence, informed decision-making becomes increasingly difficult, if not impossible. Without a shared understanding of reality, meaningful dialogue and consensus-building become elusive, hindering efforts to address pressing challenges and promote the common good.

As each piece of the puzzle falls into place, the consequences of the cultural shift in truth perception become increasingly apparent. The erosion of the notion of objective truth undermines the very foundation of democratic governance, leaving society vulnerable to manipulation and exploitation by those who seek to advance their agendas. In this environment of uncertainty and confusion, the puzzle of public discourse becomes increasingly difficult to solve, with no clear path forward.

Addressing the cultural shift in truth perception requires a concerted effort to promote media literacy, critical thinking, and a commitment to upholding the principles of truth and transparency. Like fitting together the puzzle pieces, it requires a collective willingness to challenge falsehoods and hold those in power accountable for their actions. By reaffirming the importance of objective truth and fostering a culture of truth and integrity, societies can rebuild the foundation of shared reality upon which informed decision-making relies.

Damage to Global Reputation

In the intricate puzzle of global diplomacy, Trump's use of fake news has inflicted significant damage to the United States' reputation on the global stage. Through his promotion of conspiracy theories, attacks on democratic norms, and erosion of trust in institutions, he has undermined America's credibility as a beacon of democracy and freedom. This damage to America's global reputation has weakened its ability to promote democratic values and human rights abroad, hindering efforts to address global challenges and advance peace and stability.

Imagine the damage to America's global reputation as cracks form in the puzzle of international relations, gradually widening as Trump's actions alienate allies and embolden adversaries. His promotion of conspiracy theories and attacks on democratic norms have tarnished America's image as a defender of democracy and human rights, leaving allies questioning its commitment to shared values and principles.

In this puzzle of global diplomacy, America's damaged reputation undermines its ability to promote democratic values and human rights abroad. Trump's erosion of trust in institutions and attacks on the media have weakened America's credibility as a reliable partner in the fight against authoritarianism and oppression. Without a strong foundation of trust and credibility, America's diplomatic efforts are hindered, and its ability to address global challenges is compromised.

As each piece of the puzzle falls into place, the consequences of America's damaged reputation become increasingly apparent. Allies are hesitant to align themselves with a country whose commitment to democracy and human rights is called into question. At the same time, adversaries are encouraged to challenge America's leadership on the global stage. In this environment of uncertainty and distrust, the puzzle of international relations becomes increasingly complex, with no easy solutions.

Addressing the damage to America's global reputation requires a concerted effort to reaffirm its commitment to democratic values and human rights. Like fitting together the puzzle pieces, it requires a recommitment to transparency, accountability, and respect for democratic norms. By rebuilding trust and credibility globally, America can regain its position as a leader in the fight for democracy and freedom and work toward a more peaceful and stable world.

Normalization of Authoritarian Tactics

In the puzzle of political discourse, Trump's use of fake news has led to the normalization of authoritarian tactics, such as media censorship, political repression, and the suppression of dissent. By attacking the free press as the "enemy of the people" and dismissing critical coverage as fake news, he has undermined press freedom and encouraged authoritarian leaders around the world. This normalization of authoritarian tactics poses a threat to democracy and human rights globally, as it undermines efforts to promote freedom of expression and hold authoritarian regimes accountable for their actions.

Imagine the normalization of authoritarian tactics as dark clouds gather over the puzzle of democracy, casting a shadow over the principles of freedom and human rights. Trump's attacks on the free press and his dismissal of critical coverage as fake news have created a climate of fear and intimidation, where journalists are harassed, censored, and even imprisoned for reporting the truth. In this environment, press freedom becomes a distant memory, and dissent is met with repression and violence.

In this puzzle of political repression, the normalization of authoritarian tactics poses a grave threat to democracy and human rights globally. Trump's attacks on the free press have encouraged authoritarian leaders around the world, who see his actions as a green light to crack down on dissent and silence opposition voices. As press freedom erodes and political repression intensifies, the puzzle of democracy becomes increasingly difficult to solve, with authoritarianism gaining ground and democratic values under siege.

As each piece of the puzzle falls into place, the consequences of normalizing authoritarian tactics become increasingly apparent. Journalists are harassed, imprisoned, and even killed for daring to speak truth to power. At the same time, political opponents are silenced, and dissent is stamped out. In this environment of fear and oppression, the puzzle of democracy becomes increasingly fragile, with the principles of freedom and human rights hanging in the balance.

Addressing the normalization of authoritarian tactics requires a concerted effort to defend press freedom, promote freedom of expression, and hold authoritarian regimes accountable for their actions. Like fitting together the puzzle pieces, it requires a commitment to upholding the principles of democracy and human rights, even in the face of adversity. By standing up to authoritarianism and defending the rights of journalists and political dissidents, societies can begin to dismantle the puzzle of political repression and rebuild the foundations of democracy for future generations.

Crisis of Trust in Information Sources

In the puzzle of information dissemination, Trump's use of fake news has worsened a crisis of trust in information sources, leaving individuals grappling to discern fact from fiction in an increasingly polarized and fragmented media landscape. By promoting alternative narratives and conspiracy theories, he has eroded trust in mainstream media outlets and undercut the credibility of authoritative sources of information. This crisis of trust has deepened social divisions and impeded efforts to foster a shared understanding of reality.

Picture the crisis of trust in information sources as a fog descending upon the puzzle of public perception, obscuring the distinction between truth and falsehood. Trump's relentless promotion of alternative narratives and his attacks on mainstream media have created an environment of uncertainty and doubt, where individuals are left questioning the reliability of the information they receive. In this maze of misinformation, facts become elusive, and reality becomes subjective, leading to widespread confusion and mistrust.

In this puzzle of information dissemination, the crisis of trust in information sources has fueled social divisions and hindered efforts to promote a shared understanding of reality. Trump's promotion of alternative narratives and conspiracy theories has polarized public discourse, driving individuals further apart and deepening mistrust between opposing camps. As trust in mainstream media erodes and authoritative sources of information are called into question, the puzzle of information dissemination becomes increasingly complex, with no easy solutions.

As each piece of the puzzle falls into place, the consequences of the crisis of trust in information sources become increasingly apparent. Social divisions widen, echo chambers echo louder, and efforts to bridge ideological divides falter in the face of pervasive skepticism and distrust. In this environment of uncertainty and confusion, the puzzle of public discourse becomes increasingly difficult to solve, with no clear path forward.

Addressing the crisis of trust in information sources requires a concerted effort to promote media literacy, critical thinking, and a commitment to upholding the principles of truth and transparency. Like fitting together the puzzle pieces, it requires a collective willingness to challenge falsehoods and hold those in power accountable for their actions. By reaffirming the importance of objective truth and fostering a culture of trust and integrity, societies can navigate the fog of misinformation and rebuild confidence in the information sources that form the foundation of informed decision-making.

Need for Media Literacy Education

In the puzzle of modern information consumption, Trump's use of fake news emphasizes the critical need for media literacy education. This education equips individuals with the skills to evaluate information critically and discern fact from fiction. By promoting media literacy education, societies can empower citizens to navigate the complex media landscape, identify misinformation, and make informed decisions based on reliable sources of information. Investing in media literacy education is essential for strengthening democratic governance and promoting a culture of truth and transparency.

Imagine the need for media literacy education as a beacon of light, illuminating the puzzle of information dissemination and guiding individuals through the maze of misinformation and disinformation. Trump's use of fake news has underscored the importance of equipping individuals with the tools to critically assess the credibility and reliability of the information they encounter. In this era of digital media and social networks, media literacy education is more crucial than ever, enabling individuals to navigate the flood of information and distinguish between fact and falsehood.

In this puzzle of information consumption, media literacy education empowers citizens to become active participants in the media landscape rather than passive information consumers. By teaching critical thinking skills, source evaluation techniques, and fact-checking methods, media literacy education enables individuals to discern between credible and unreliable sources of information. Doing so fosters a culture of skepticism and inquiry, where truth is valued over sensationalism and misinformation.

As each piece of the puzzle falls into place, the benefits of media literacy education become increasingly apparent. Citizens are better equipped to identify misinformation and propaganda, resist manipulation by vested interests, and make informed decisions based on evidence and facts. In this media literacy environment, the information dissemination puzzle becomes more transparent, with truth and transparency guiding the way forward.

Addressing the need for media literacy education requires a concerted effort from policymakers, educators, and civil society organizations. By integrating media literacy into school curricula, promoting public awareness campaigns, and providing resources for lifelong learning, societies can empower citizens to navigate the complex media landscape and become responsible consumers and creators of information. This investment in media literacy education is essential for strengthening democratic governance, promoting informed citizenship, and safeguarding the integrity of public discourse in an age of information abundance.

Threat to Democratic Institutions

In the intricate puzzle of democratic governance, Trump's use of fake news posed a significant threat to democratic institutions, including the separation of powers and the rule of law. By undermining public trust in institutions such as the judiciary and law enforcement, he weakened the checks and balances essential for holding elected officials accountable. This erosion of democratic institutions undermined the foundations of democracy. It posed a danger to the stability and integrity of the political system.

Imagine the threat to democratic institutions as cracks forming in the puzzle of governance, weakening the structure that upholds the principles of democracy and the rule of law. Trump's attacks on the judiciary and law enforcement, coupled with his promotion of false narratives and conspiracy theories, eroded public trust in these vital institutions. In doing so, he undermined the checks and balances meant to prevent the abuse of power and hold elected officials accountable to the people they serve.

In this puzzle of democratic governance, the erosion of trust in institutions poses a grave threat to the stability and integrity of the political system. Without a judiciary that is perceived as independent and impartial and law enforcement agencies that are trusted to uphold the rule of law, democracy becomes vulnerable to authoritarianism and tyranny. Trump's use of fake news further weakened the foundations of democracy, leaving the puzzle of governance increasingly fragile and susceptible to manipulation.

As each piece of the puzzle falls into place, the consequences of the threat to democratic institutions become increasingly apparent. The erosion of public trust in key institutions undermines the effectiveness of democratic governance, as citizens lose faith in the ability of their government to serve their interests and protect their rights. In this environment of uncertainty and distrust, the puzzle of democratic governance becomes increasingly difficult to solve, with no clear path forward.

Addressing the threat to democratic institutions requires a concerted effort to rebuild public trust and strengthen the checks and balances essential for maintaining a healthy democracy. Like fitting together the pieces of a puzzle, it requires a commitment to upholding the rule of law, promoting transparency and accountability, and defending the independence of key institutions. By reaffirming the importance of democratic principles and institutions, societies can begin to repair the damage inflicted by Trump's attacks and safeguard the integrity of democratic governance for future generations.

Influence on Public Policy

In the intricate puzzle of governance, Trump's use of fake news profoundly influenced public policy decisions and government actions, shaping the direction of both domestic and foreign policy. He manipulated public opinion by promoting false narratives and conspiracy theories and pressured policymakers to adopt his agenda. This manipulation of public opinion undermined evidence-based policymaking and hindered efforts to address pressing issues such as climate change, healthcare reform, and economic inequality.

Imagine the influence on public policy as a powerful force guiding the puzzle pieces of governance, shaping the decisions that impact the lives of millions. Trump's use of fake news, coupled with his mastery of media manipulation, enabled him to control the narrative and sway public opinion in favor of his policies and initiatives. Through fear-mongering, misinformation, and conspiracy theories, he rallied his base. He pressured policymakers to prioritize his agenda over evidence-based solutions.

In this puzzle of governance, the influence of fake news on public policy decisions undermined the principles of evidence-based policymaking and rational discourse. Trump's promotion of false narratives and conspiracy theories distorted public perception, making it difficult for policymakers to craft informed and effective policies. Issues such as climate change, healthcare reform, and economic inequality became politicized battlegrounds, with truth and evidence falling victim to partisan agendas.

As each piece of the puzzle falls into place, the consequences of the influence on public policy become increasingly apparent. Evidence-based policymaking gives way to political expediency, as policymakers prioritize short-term gains over long-term solutions. The governance puzzle becomes increasingly fragmented, with partisan divisions deepening and efforts to address pressing challenges hampered by misinformation and political polarization.

Addressing the influence on public policy requires a concerted effort to promote media literacy, critical thinking, and a commitment to evidence-based decision-making. Like fitting together the puzzle pieces, it requires a recommitment to truth and transparency in public discourse and a willingness to challenge falsehoods and misinformation wherever they arise. By reaffirming the importance of evidence-based policymaking and promoting a culture of informed citizenship, societies can begin to untangle the knots of misinformation and chart a course toward effective and equitable governance for all.

Cultural Impact on Truth and Integrity

In the intricate tapestry of societal values, Trump's use of fake news has woven a profound cultural impact on how truth and integrity are perceived and valued in society. By normalizing dishonesty and deception in public discourse, he undermined the values of honesty and transparency essential for maintaining a healthy democracy. This cultural shift in attitudes toward truth and integrity has eroded the moral fabric of society and undermined the social norms that govern ethical behavior.

Imagine the cultural impact on truth and integrity as cracks form in the foundation of societal values, weakening the bonds that hold communities together. Trump's use of fake news, coupled with his disregard for truth and transparency, has eroded public trust in institutions and undermined the credibility of authoritative sources of information. In this environment of moral ambiguity, truth becomes subjective, and integrity becomes a relic of the past, replaced by a culture of deception and dishonesty.

In this tapestry of societal values, the cultural impact of fake news has far-reaching consequences for the fabric of democracy. Trump's normalization of dishonesty and deception has eroded public trust in the institutions that form the foundation of democratic governance, leaving society vulnerable to manipulation and exploitation by those seeking to advance their agendas. As truth and integrity are sacrificed on the altar of political expediency, society's moral compass becomes increasingly skewed, with ethical behavior becoming a casualty of partisan warfare.

As each tapestry thread falls into place, the consequences of the cultural impact on truth and integrity become increasingly apparent. Social norms that once governed ethical behavior are eroded and replaced by a culture of cynicism and distrust. In this environment of moral relativism, the tapestry of societal values becomes increasingly frayed, with no clear path forward.

Addressing the cultural impact on truth and integrity requires a concerted effort to reaffirm the importance of honesty, transparency, and ethical behavior in public discourse and governance. Like weaving together the threads of a tapestry, it requires a commitment to upholding the values that form the foundation of a healthy democracy. By promoting a culture of truth and integrity, societies can begin to mend the cracks in the moral fabric of society and rebuild trust in the institutions that form the bedrock of democratic governance.

Damage to Social Cohesion

In the intricate web of societal bonds, Trump's use of fake news has inflicted significant damage to social cohesion, exacerbating divisions and undermining unity among Americans. By promoting conspiracy theories and demonizing political opponents, he fueled resentment and distrust among different segments of society, pitting Americans against each other along ideological lines. This damage to social cohesion has undermined efforts to promote unity and inclusivity, hindering progress toward a more harmonious and equitable society.

Imagine the damage to social cohesion as cracks form in the foundation of societal bonds, weakening the ties that bind communities. Trump's use of fake news, coupled with his divisive rhetoric, has deepened existing divisions and sowed seeds of distrust and hatred among Americans. In this fractured landscape, unity becomes elusive, and inclusivity becomes a distant dream as individuals retreat into their respective ideological echo chambers.

In this web of societal bonds, the damage to social cohesion undermines efforts to bridge divides and foster a sense of belonging and solidarity. Trump's promotion of conspiracy theories and demonization of political opponents has polarized public discourse, making it increasingly difficult for individuals to engage in constructive dialogue and find common ground. As social divisions deepen and trust erodes, the fabric of society becomes increasingly frayed, with unity and inclusivity giving way to division and discord.

As each strand of the web falls into place, the consequences of the damage to social cohesion become increasingly apparent. Communities become fragmented, with individuals retreating into ideological bubbles and dismissing opposing viewpoints as fake news. In this environment of polarization and distrust, efforts to promote unity and inclusivity falter, leaving society divided and adrift.

Addressing the damage to social cohesion requires a concerted effort to bridge divides and foster a sense of common purpose and belonging. Like repairing the strands of a frayed web, it requires a commitment to promoting empathy, understanding, and respect for diversity. By challenging divisive rhetoric and promoting constructive dialogue, societies can begin to mend the cracks in the foundation of societal bonds and build a more harmonious and equitable future for all.

Need for Democratic Renewal

In the wake of Trump's use of fake news, a call for democratic renewal emerges—a call to action to strengthen democratic governance and promote accountability and transparency in government. By addressing the root causes of disinformation and rebuilding trust in institutions, societies can reclaim the values of democracy and truth essential for safeguarding the rights and freedoms of all citizens. This commitment to democratic renewal is crucial for overcoming the legacy of fake news and building a more resilient and inclusive democracy for future generations.

Imagine the need for democratic renewal as a beacon of hope shining through the fog of misinformation, guiding societies toward a brighter future.

Trump's use of fake news has laid bare the vulnerabilities of democratic governance, exposing the cracks in the foundation of truth and transparency. In this moment of reckoning, societies have an opportunity to recommit to the values that form the bedrock of democracy—values such as accountability, transparency, and respect for the rule of law.

In this journey toward democratic renewal, societies must confront the root causes of disinformation and distrust that have plagued public discourse. By promoting media literacy, critical thinking, and civic engagement, societies can empower citizens to navigate the complex media landscape and discern fact from fiction. Additionally, by strengthening democratic institutions, promoting transparency in government, and holding elected officials accountable for their actions, societies can rebuild trust and confidence in the democratic process.

As each step toward democratic renewal is taken, the path forward becomes more apparent, and the promise of a more resilient and inclusive democracy comes into focus. By reaffirming the importance of democratic principles and values, societies can overcome the legacy of fake news and build a future where truth and integrity prevail. In this renewed commitment to democracy lies the hope for a brighter tomorrow—a tomorrow where the rights and freedoms of all citizens are upheld, and the promise of democracy is realized for generations to come.

Addressing the need for democratic renewal requires a collective effort from all sectors of society—government, civil society, and the media. By working together to promote accountability, transparency, and trust in institutions, societies can overcome the challenges of fake news and build a more robust, more resilient democracy for the future. With a renewed commitment to democratic principles and values, societies can chart a course toward a brighter future where truth and integrity guide the way forward.

Donald Trump's utilization of fake news during his presidential campaigns and tenure in office has had profound and far-reaching consequences for American democracy and global politics. From the erosion of trust in information sources to the normalization of authoritarian tactics and the damage to America's global reputation, his use of fake news has left a lasting impact on the fabric of society. Addressing the proliferation of fake news will require concerted efforts to rebuild trust, promote media literacy education, and uphold the values of democracy and truth.

Trump's reliance on fake news as a political tool has fundamentally altered the landscape of American democracy. By undermining trust in information sources and promoting alternative narratives, he has eroded the foundation of truth upon which democratic governance relies. Normalizing fake news tactics has further polarized an already divided society, deepening social divisions and hindering efforts to promote unity and inclusivity.

Moreover, Trump's use of fake news has had ripple effects on the global stage, tarnishing America's reputation as a beacon of democracy and freedom. His attacks on democratic institutions and the promotion of conspiracy theories have encouraged authoritarian leaders around the world, undermining efforts to promote human rights and democratic values globally. The damage to America's global reputation will require sustained efforts to rebuild trust and credibility internationally.

Addressing the proliferation of fake news will require a multifaceted approach that tackles the root causes of misinformation and promotes media literacy education. By empowering citizens to critically evaluate information and discern fact from fiction, societies can mitigate the impact of fake news and strengthen the resilience of democratic institutions. Additionally, upholding the values of democracy and truth is essential for safeguarding the integrity of public discourse and promoting informed citizenship.

In conclusion, the proliferation of fake news poses a significant threat to democratic governance and societal cohesion. Trump's use of fake news has underscored the urgent need for action to address this challenge and uphold the principles of democracy and truth. By rebuilding trust, promoting media literacy education, and defending the values of democracy, societies can confront the legacy of fake news and build a more resilient and inclusive future for all.

Preventing Another Insurrection

Preventing another insurrection is crucial for several reasons, impacting the stability, security, and integrity of a nation. An insurrection undermines democratic institutions and the rule of law, threatening the very foundation of governance and citizens' trust in their government. It can lead to significant violence and destruction, putting lives at risk and causing extensive damage to public and private property. The economic consequences can be severe, deterring investment and disrupting businesses, thereby harming the livelihoods of many. Furthermore, such unrest exacerbates social and political divisions, making it harder to achieve national unity and cooperation. On an international level, a nation experiencing insurrection loses credibility, weakening its global standing and diplomatic relations. By preventing insurrections, we ensure that differences are resolved through peaceful dialogue and democratic processes, maintaining a stable, secure, and unified society that upholds the principles of justice, fairness, and respect for all.

Protecting Democracy

Upholding Democratic Institutions

Upholding democratic institutions is essential for maintaining the stability and legitimacy of a government. An insurrection threatens the very foundation of these institutions, which are designed to operate based on the rule of law and the will of the people. Democratic institutions, such as the legislature, judiciary, and executive branches, provide checks and balances that ensure no single entity or group holds too much power. This balance is crucial for protecting individual freedoms, maintaining justice, and ensuring that all voices are heard in the governance process. When an insurrection occurs, it disrupts these institutions, undermining their ability to function effectively and eroding public trust in their legitimacy. Protecting democratic institutions from such threats ensures that laws are created, interpreted, and enforced fairly and consistently. It also guarantees that elected officials are accountable to the people, making decisions that reflect the collective will of the electorate. By upholding these institutions, we preserve the integrity of the democratic process, fostering a stable and just society where power is exercised responsibly and citizens can confidently participate in their government.

Ensuring Fair Elections

Ensuring fair elections is fundamental to the health and legitimacy of a democracy. Preventing insurrection is critical to maintaining the integrity of these elections, ensuring they are free, fair, and respected by all citizens. Fair elections rely on the peaceful transition of power and the assurance that every vote counts and is counted accurately. Insurrections disrupt this process by introducing violence and coercion, which can intimidate voters, suppress turnout, and compromise the security of election infrastructure. When elections are threatened by such unrest, the public's confidence in the electoral process diminishes, leading to doubts about the legitimacy of the outcomes and weakening the overall democratic framework.

By preventing insurrections, we protect the right of every citizen to participate in choosing their leaders without fear of violence or intimidation. This safeguards the principles of one person, one vote, ensuring that elections are conducted transparently and that results reflect the true will of the people. Moreover, preventing insurrections helps maintain a stable environment where electoral authorities can operate independently and free from external pressures, further enhancing the credibility of the electoral process. In turn, this fosters greater public trust and acceptance of election outcomes, promoting political stability and continuity. Ensuring fair elections through the prevention of insurrections ultimately strengthens democracy by affirming the core values of political participation, representation, and accountability.

Safeguarding Public Safety

Preventing Violence and Harm

Insurrections often lead to violence, resulting in injuries or loss of life. By preventing such events, we protect people from harm.

Maintaining Order

Ensuring peace and order prevents chaos and destruction, preserving public and private property and the well-being of communities.

Promoting National Unity

Fostering National Unity

Preventing insurrections helps avoid deepening divisions within society, fostering a sense of unity and common purpose among citizens.

Encouraging Peaceful Dialogue

When insurrections are prevented, it encourages people to engage in peaceful and constructive dialogue to resolve differences.

Economic Stability

Ensuring Economic Stability

Political violence and instability can negatively impact the economy by deterring investment, disrupting business operations, and increasing the costs of security and recovery.

Protecting Jobs and Livelihoods

Preventing insurrections ensures that businesses can operate smoothly, protecting jobs and the livelihoods of many people.

Preserving International Reputation

Maintaining International Credibility

A stable and peaceful nation is respected on the global stage, which is essential for maintaining strong international relations and cooperation.

Attracting Foreign Investment

Stability and a strong rule of law attract foreign investment, contributing to economic growth and development.

Legal and Ethical Responsibilities

Enforcing the Rule of Law

Preventing insurrections ensures that the rule of law is upheld, holding individuals accountable for unlawful actions and deterring future attempts at violent upheaval.

Protecting Civil Rights

By preventing insurrections, the government can better protect the civil rights and liberties of all citizens, ensuring they are not violated during periods of unrest.

Social Cohesion

Reducing Polarization

Efforts to prevent insurrections can help address and mitigate political and social polarization, fostering a more inclusive and cohesive society.

Building Trust in Government

Effective prevention and response to threats help build and maintain public trust in government institutions and their ability to protect and serve the populace.

Encouraging Responsible Leadership

Promoting Accountable Leadership

Leaders who work to prevent insurrections demonstrate responsible and accountable governance, setting a positive example for citizens and future leaders.

Preventing Radicalization

Addressing the underlying causes of discontent can prevent radicalization and the spread of extremist ideologies that often lead to insurrections.

Long-term Stability

Ensuring Long-term Stability

By addressing the root causes of political unrest and taking preventive measures, a nation can ensure long-term stability and peace.

Strengthening Institutions

Preventing insurrections involves strengthening institutions and processes that uphold democracy, making them more resilient to future threats.

Preserving the Foundations of Democracy

Protecting the Constitution

An insurrection challenges the principles enshrined in the Constitution. Preventing such events ensures that constitutional rights and the balance of powers are upheld.

Ensuring Legislative Function

The legislative branch must operate without the threat of violence to create laws that reflect the people's will.

Promoting Civic Engagement

Encouraging Civic Participation

A peaceful and stable society encourages more citizens to engage in civic activities, such as voting and community involvement.

Building a Culture of Respect

Preventing insurrections helps foster a culture of respect for democratic processes and institutions, which is essential for their long-term sustainability.

Enhancing Security Measures

Strengthening National Security

Preventing insurrections is a critical aspect of national security, protecting the nation from internal threats that can weaken it.

Preventing Terrorism

Effective measures against insurrections also help prevent domestic terrorism and other forms of violent extremism.

Supporting Mental Health and Well-being

Reducing Stress and Anxiety

Political violence creates stress and anxiety among the populace. Preventing insurrections helps maintain mental well-being.

Providing Stability for Future Generations

Ensuring a stable and peaceful society is essential for the mental and emotional well-being of future generations.

Encouraging Responsible Media

Promoting Responsible Journalism

Preventing insurrections encourages media outlets to report responsibly, avoiding sensationalism that can incite violence.

Combating Misinformation

Efforts to prevent insurrections include combating misinformation and disinformation that can fuel unrest.

Upholding Ethical Standards

Maintaining Moral Integrity

Upholding the law and preventing insurrections demonstrates a commitment to moral and ethical standards in governance.

Encouraging Ethical Behavior

A society that values and enforces laws encourages ethical behavior among its citizens.

Protecting Human Rights

Ensuring Human Rights

Insurrections often lead to human rights abuses. Preventing them protects the fundamental rights and freedoms of all individuals.

Promoting Justice and Fairness

A society that prevents insurrections is one that values justice and fairness, ensuring that grievances are addressed through lawful means.

Fostering International Cooperation

Strengthening Alliances

A stable nation is better positioned to strengthen alliances and engage in meaningful international cooperation.

Supporting Global Peace

Preventing insurrections contributes to global peace and security by setting an example for other nations.

Economic Growth and Prosperity

Promoting Long-term Economic Growth

Stability attracts long-term investments, leading to sustained economic growth and prosperity.

Protecting Infrastructure

Preventing insurrections protects critical infrastructure from damage and destruction, ensuring the smooth functioning of society.

Encouraging Innovation and Progress

Fostering Innovation

A stable and secure environment encourages innovation and progress, as people feel safe to explore new ideas and ventures.

Supporting Education

Stability ensures that educational institutions can operate without disruption, promoting learning and development.

Enhancing Community Resilience

Building Strong Communities

Preventing insurrections fosters strong, resilient communities that can withstand and recover from crises.

Promoting Social Cohesion

Efforts to prevent insurrections enhance social cohesion, creating a more harmonious and cooperative society.

Demonstrating Global Leadership

Setting a Positive Example

By effectively preventing insurrections, a nation sets a positive example of governance and stability for the world.

Contributing to International Norms

A stable and democratic nation contributes to the establishment and maintenance of international norms and standards.

Ensuring Accountability

Holding Perpetrators Accountable

Preventing insurrections involves holding those responsible for inciting or participating in violence accountable for their actions.

Strengthening Legal Frameworks

Ensuring that legal frameworks are robust and capable of addressing and preventing insurrections is critical for accountability.

Promoting Inclusive Governance

Ensuring Representation

Preventing insurrections promotes inclusive governance, where all groups feel represented and heard.

Addressing Inequality

Efforts to prevent insurrections often include addressing social and economic inequalities that can fuel discontent.

Fostering National Pride

Building National Pride

A peaceful and stable nation fosters a sense of pride and patriotism among its citizens.

Celebrating Democratic Values

Preventing insurrections allows a nation to celebrate and uphold its democratic values and traditions.

Ensuring Resilient Leadership

Promoting Resilient Leadership

Leaders who effectively prevent insurrections demonstrate resilience and the ability to guide the nation through challenges.

Strengthening Crisis Management

Efforts to prevent insurrections strengthen the nation's overall crisis management capabilities.

In conclusion, preventing another insurrection is essential for preserving democracy, ensuring public safety, promoting national unity, and fostering a stable and prosperous society. It requires a comprehensive approach that addresses the root causes of discontent, strengthens institutions, and promotes a culture of peace and respect for the rule of law.

Don't miss out!

Visit the website below and you can sign up to receive emails whenever Adrian Rocquecliffe publishes a new book. There's no charge and no obligation.

https://books2read.com/r/B-A-LUNRB-CYCSD

BOOKS 2 READ

Connecting independent readers to independent writers.

Did you love *Trump's Insurrection of the US Capitol*? Then you should read *Making America Great Altogether - Call to Action*[1] by Adrian Rocquecliffe!

[2]

In our rallying cry, 'Making America Great Altogether – Call to Action,' unity takes center stage but with a twist. Instead of pushing for uniformity, we celebrate the vibrant patchwork of perspectives that make up our nation. It's about inclusivity, where every voice, no matter how different, is not just heard but cherished. This is not just a call. It's an invitation to be part of something bigger.

This call for unity recognizes that diversity isn't just a buzzword—it's the lifeblood of progress. By weaving together the varied threads of American society, we create a tapestry of resilience and innovation. Whether you're from a bustling city or a quiet country town, whether your roots trace back generations or you're a newcomer, your voice matters. You are an integral part of this collective progress.

---

1. https://books2read.com/u/mK25PP

2. https://books2read.com/u/mK25PP

But it's not just about warm fuzzies; it's practical, too. In a world where challenges come fast and furious, we need all hands on deck. By embracing our differences and fostering a culture of openness, we tap into a wellspring of creativity and insight that can steer us through even the toughest of times.

Let's ditch the divisiveness and roll out the welcome mat for all. In "Making America Great Altogether," we're not just talking the talk; we're walking the walk toward a future where everyone has a seat at the table.

Read more at https://www.makingamericagreataltogether.us/adrian_rocquecliffe.

Also by Adrian Rocquecliffe

Making America Great Altogether - Call to Action
Trump's Vision of MAGA- The Fallacy
Extra! Extra! Read All About It
Trump's Insurrection of the US Capitol
How Well do you Know Your Candidate?
Trumpisms: Decoding the Rhetoric of Disruption
The Republican Agenda: Undoing 200 Years of Democracy for a Dictatorship
Under the Iron Flag: A Family's Battle for Survival and Justice in Trump's America
Complimentary Orchiectomy with First Sexual Offense: Starting at the Top
The Gulf of America: Trump's Vision for a United Continent
Project 2026 USA: We the People, For the People, By the People

Watch for more at https://www.makingamericagreataltogether.us/
adrian_rocquecliffe.

About the Author

Adrian Rocquecliffe's journey from a young boy navigating cultural divides to a successful entrepreneur and visionary leader exemplifies the American dream. His dedication to improving the country for future generations is a testament to his belief in the power of unity and collaboration. As he continues his work with "Making America Great Altogether," Adrian remains hopeful that his efforts will contribute to a better, more inclusive America when he retires.

Read more at https://www.makingamericagreataltogether.us/ adrian_rocquecliffe.

About the Publisher

Writers Sidekick Publishing is a key part of the Writers Sidekick Resource Hub. Writers Sidekick Publishing specializes in publishing anthologies that welcome submissions from both new and established authors, providing a platform to showcase their work and contribute to the literary world. Additionally, it produces exclusive books tailored to the needs of the Writers Sidekick Resource Hub community.